Thureeyam

Kundalini Secret

(Yogic Science)

M. Devarajan

Spiritual Guidance Society
Bunglow Kunnu, Kongad P.O., Palakkad, Kerala – 678 631
Contact: 9895610455

After a long teaching career, retired from service in 2022. Has been practicing and teaching Yoga for four decades. Is trained in Tibettan Yoga, Chinese Thai Chi, Kalarippayattu, Karate etc. Now focus on propagating the benefits of Yoga and Pranayama through classes and discourses, with a specialized focus on treating depression through therapeutic yoga.

Thureeyam

Kundalini Secret

(Yogic Science)

M. Devarajan

English

THUREEYAM - KUNDALINI SECRET

(Yogic Science)

Author:

M. Devarajan

Ph : 98956 10455

Translation :

K. Mohanan, Palakkad

Published on: 2026 March

Cover & Illustration:

Kannan Image, Palakkd

ISBN : 978-93-5812-372-2

Pre press:

Ashok Classic, PKD

Printing:

Price: INR

Publisher:

Spiritual Guidance Society

Thureeyam Kundalini Secret – Yogic Science

Bunglawkunnu, Kongad

Palakkad - 678631

Youtube : spiritual guidance society

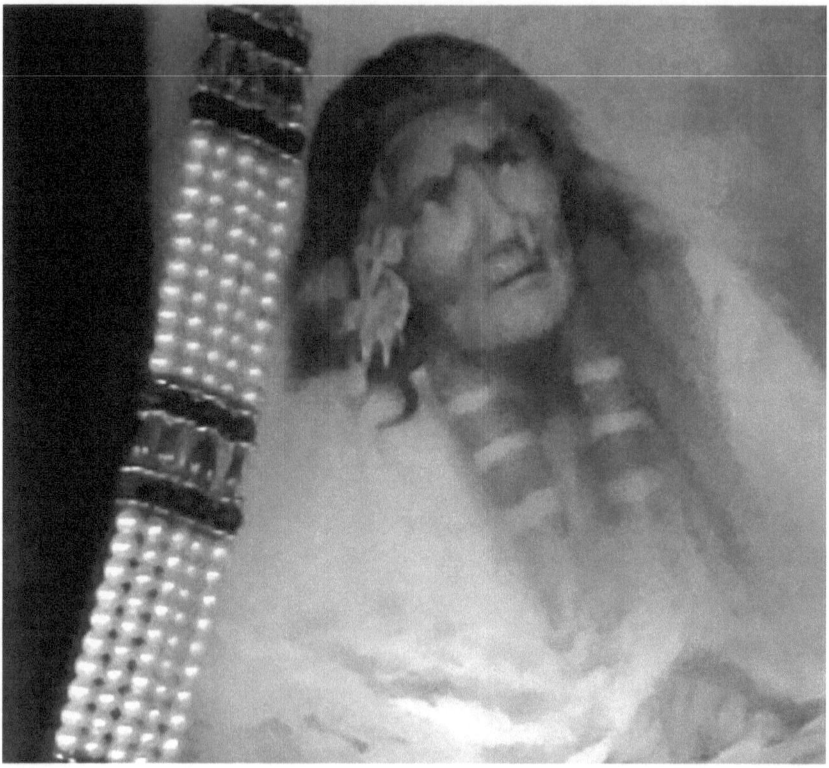

Thiruvallam Amma
Avadhootha Kudi, Karumam,
Thiruvananthapuram

Remembering with gratitude the subtle presence of Amma who guided me throughout the writing of this book.

Foreword

Yoga is the most glorious legacy India has shared to humanity. Archaeological and textual evidence trace the practice of yoga in India back over thousands of years. We understand that Yoga has been widely adopted as a holistic practice for optimizing physical, mental, and spiritual wellness by a large section of people.

The common, but incomplete, view of yoga is that of a purely physical, stretching-focused workout. Because yoga was popularized globally primarily through one of its eight limbs—Asanas (physical postures)—a narrow, fitness-focused perception of yoga spread worldwide. While India rightly takes pride in being the birthplace of Yoga and its many sages, few truly dive deep into its philosophy to uncover the hidden secrets of the practice. Yoga is rarely utilized in its entirety - as a means for enhancing well-being, cultivating joy, and attaining the final human goal of liberation - and is instead confined to a method of physical exercise.

Despite boasting a foundational, universal body of traditional knowledge, India historically maintained an insular, secretive, and hierarchical method of knowledge transfer that was exclusive to a privileged few. Nevertheless, the impact of these traditions was profound enough to earn universal acknowledgment. Consequently, access to knowledge was restricted to the elite class.

However, a positive shift has occurred in the recent past. Today, any seeker with sincere commitment and curiosity can master yoga and uncover its hidden secrets. Through a combination of expert training and digital platforms, yoga has become widely accessible to a global audience.

There is a shift toward integrating traditional yogic practices into modern higher education curricula. More than that, with the help of Masters, anyone can begin their journey into the world of yoga. Most of the practitioners resort to this for personalized, relaxed guidance or to receive focused one-on-one support. Dedicated practitioners frequently pursue further study through yoga literature and research. "The Yoga Sutras", written by Sage Patanjali, is a text that seekers can use for serious study. Although hundreds of books are available detailing yoga methods and mysteries, the 'Yogasutra' is the one followed by most for its authenticity. Because the original text is in Sanskrit, we must rely on commentaries in regional languages.

Because the Yoga Sutras present concepts in concise aphorisms (sutras), common people must rely on explanations in vernacular languages (commentaries) to understand them. It is true that interpretations of the sutras seem to differ with every commentator. By synthesizing different commentaries with my own observations, I have developed a simple, direct approach to explaining the mysteries of Yoga, ensuring they are easily understood by everyone.

This small handbook is offered at the feet of the Acharya, with a prayer that it will help you directly grasp the core mysteries of Yoga and reach your ultimate goal by understanding and practicing its principles.

M. Devarajan

From Chittākāśa to Chidākāśa: The Inner Meanings of Yogic Testimonies

Biju Sarada Padmanabhan

What is the meaning of this inevitable moment? What is this existence itself? Amid the turbulent tides of birth and death, when one pauses briefly to gaze at the stillness of the shore, there arises within the depths of that seeker a fleeting wonder—a mystical amazement shaped by existentialism and absurdity. When the search goes for finding the very meaning of life in this transient, illusory world one becomes totally hapless. This cause of this cosmic drama ought to be the undeniable inner call of every conscious being. We witness a biological blindness that dissolves itself in mere fascination with transformations seen around. Is this blindness innate, or is it acquired? O Supreme Radiance that transcends all darkness—my prostrations to You!

The tension that lies between what is seen and unseen, heard and unheard is the silent witness to the profound contemplation expressed in the idea that clearly emerges from darkness. From doing nothing at all to undertake the most arduous spiritual pursuit, it becomes evident that there is no single absolute method.

A story of Sage Nārada bears testimony to this truth. When the great devotee Nārada learned that several more births still remained before liberation, the disappointment he felt was transferred to a man he encountered on the way. That man was lost in a trance-like state, swinging joyfully on a tamarind tree, immersed in the play of his own thoughts. When he asked Nārada about his liberation, the sage replied irritatingly that he will attain moksha only after many lifetime equalling the number of leaves on the tree he was sitting. Upon hearing this, the man burst into ecstatic joy, proclaiming that even if it took countless lifetimes, he was not rejected—his liberation was assured. Soon he received Moksha.

It is at this precise juncture that the arrival of "Turīyam – The Alchemy of Awakening Consciousness" by Manikandan Devarajan becomes profoundly relevant. The non-human yet supra-human revelations of light offer immense solace to the weary traveller. We have remained distant, far too long from the sacred landscapes of self-awareness where knowledge once blossomed during mantra-filled moments of inner awakening. From the five elements to the supreme consciousness of Sadāśiva, the majestic uniqueness of the thirty-six tattvas unfolds. These errant journeys—filled with disorder, intricate configurations, and constant reconfigurations—can bewilder the seeker until their deeper patterns are understood. In such a context, this work fulfills its ethical and spiritual responsibility with remarkable clarity. As Swami Vivekananda perceived it, yoga is a confluence of Eastern and Western thought. The phenomenon of the mind—still an unsolved puzzle for modern sciences—can be comprehended fully only through yogic science.

In truth, Yoga science is Indian psychology. Only when this is understood do we realize that yoga is the profound alchemy that recognizes consciousness and mind accurately, disciplines the mind, and awakens awareness. One whose consciousness has awakened is a Buddha.There is no doubt that this concise book offers powerful illumination to awaken the wisdom-consciousness within you. The book presents exceptional explorations into the hidden Kundalini energy, the experiential awakening achieved through Kundalini Yoga, and transformations of consciousness explained through authentic nāḍī (energy-channel) sciences. These elements make the book indispensable.

Although the six chakras and their functions are widely discussed across various levels, Manikandan Devarajan's explanations provide a uniquely lucid and unparalleled perspective. The precision and subtlety with which the ascending and descending flows of energy through the chakras are described are remarkable. The traits and potential of the sthita-prajña (one established in wisdom) are presented in a way that even a common reader can grasp. Samādhi and arūpa-samādhi are portrayed not as distant ideals but as attainable states achieved through natural inner mastery.

This is the living vision of "Turīyam – The Alchemy of Awakening Consciousness." Among books of similar genre, this work stands apart in both conceptual richness and presentation. Moving away from the dry prose of academic texts, the poetic continuity of its language makes the reading deeply engaging. By integrating diverse spiritual practices, the author skillfully dissolves the seeker's inner anxieties and elevates them toward the grandeur of wisdom. One can sense that profound interventions have shaped this work—perhaps through parallel journeys across similar traditions—creating a harmonious unity of ideas.

In several places, conventional notions are dismantled through striking reinterpretations. Distortions within sacred spaces, misdirected exchanges of spiritual energies, and ritualistic confusions are examined as lived experiences, offering clear resolutions to the seeker's doubts. "The central ground of the Triveni Sangam" emerges as an astonishing grace bestowed by the divine.

This small yet powerful work serves as a guiding light for anyone wishing to traverse the subtle domains of yogic science without faltering, ultimately enabling a vision of chidākāśa (the space of pure consciousness). In these intensely materialistic times, may this book become a beacon for sincere spiritual seekers.

May the author be blessed to weave further insights into this work through deeper inner revelations.

Destiny will ensure that this book reaches only the hands of those who truly seek. The Urim and Thummim within the seeker will naturally draw them toward it.

With gratitude for the merit that allowed me to be part of this journey, I present this work to awakened minds.

With love and reverence,
Biju Sarada Padmanabhan
Psychic Investigator,
Influencer @ Esp Paranormal

CONTENT

YOGASUTRA

Just as Newton and Einstein revolutionized our understanding of the physical universe, Sage Patanjali acted as a pioneering scientist of the inner world, mapping the depths of human consciousness. Patanjali's Yoga Sutras provide a detailed, step-by-step roadmap for achieving the highest state of spiritual liberation (paramapadam) through disciplined, systematic practice. Following the path set by the Master is all a seeker needs to do. Following His instructions guarantees reaching the final state of liberation. Rarely has another literary work explained spirituality with such clarity and scientific precision. Concepts of yoga has been well documented by him, in a concise form (soothram) eliminating unwanted explanations and details. That is why it is known as yogasuthra .

However, understanding the Yoga Sutras and unlocking their hidden mysteries has become challenging for the common man. Various reasons explain this scenario. Only by identifying and overcoming them can we truly dive into the mysteries of the yogasutra.

The foremost reason that can be ascribed is that, Yogasuthra is a theoretical work. This work provides a detailed explanation of matters related to your inner condition and mysteries of the spiritual path. It covers the definition of yoga and liberation, essential practices for achieving Absolute freedom (Kaivalya), and the signs of spiritual awakening. All these are explained in a very subtle manner; even though, Yogasuthra is not a system that teaches the methods to achieve greater heights in the field of spirituality. While it explains the theory in detail, it fails to elaborate on the methods. This must be acquired directly from a Master, not just by studying the Yoga Sutras. For a disciple learning directly from the Master, studying the Yoga Sutras provides an added tool to gain in-depth knowledge and insight into the methods being followed. Unlike the Hatha Yoga Pradipika or Yoga Yajnavalkya, which offer direct, physical instructions, the Yoga Sutras is primarily a philosophical guide for the mind rather than a practical manual.

Since Yogasuthra is not a practical way of doing kriyas, mere reading will not help one to master the techniques or learn the intricate inner secrets hidden in the book. However, for those who have acquired knowledge directly from a Master, reading this text will deepen their insight into the esoteric concepts. As practitioners follow the Master's guidance and enjoy the fruits of their efforts, they become illuminated by each sutra. Ultimately, the depth of one's involvement determines the extent of their understanding. Given the subtle, capsule form of this work, the technical language of a single sutra requires cross-referencing with its application in other contexts and literature. One can only ascertain the true level and significance of these sutras by comparing them with the detailed explanations found in other yoga texts. Therefore, the subjects discussed in this work are compared with explanations from various yoga texts. Beyond restricting a seeker to the Yogasutra, this work provides an in-depth study of other essential texts and the teachings of various Acharyas to ensure a comprehensive understanding of mandatory knowledge.

Methods of Yoga

The term yoga signifies the union of the individual self (the embodied soul, or Atman) with the universal consciousness (the Ultimate Reality, or Paramatma), which is considered the fundamental source of the creation of the Universe. This concept represents the ultimate spiritual goal of achieving complete oneness and liberation. Indian philosophical traditions articulate a concept where every individual soul (Atman) originates from the eternal source known as Brahman.This soul is understood to undergo a cycle of transmigration (samsara), inhabiting various forms, including plants and animals, across countless existences before finally achieving a human birth. This journey is often depicted as a process of spiritual evolution and purification through different life forms. The spiritual belief is that the individual soul (atma) undergoes a cycle of existence through countless rebirths, ultimately seeking to reunite with its divine origin. To achieve natural liberation (moksha), the soul is believed to require embodiment over millions of life cycles. The nature of a person's rebirth, whether as noble or abject, is determined by the karma they accrue in each life. Performing noble actions results in positive karma, thereby paving the way for a more noble existence in the future. Evil actions result in a more miserable life than his current one. Liberation is achieved through the cessation of new karmic activity and the depletion of accumulated karmic results. Consequently, the soul experiences an extended journey through the cycle of births and deaths.

Yoga is the path to achieving spiritual liberation (moksha), freeing the soul from the cycle of worldly existence.

The practice and mastery of yoga aim to achieve moksha, freeing one from the perpetual cycle of births and deaths. He is now in a liberated state, an extraordinary achievement that typically requires innumerable lifetimes of spiritual practice. A yogi achieves liberation in this life itself (jivanmukta) by utilizing advanced practices (yoga) to dismantle the latent behavioral patterns and karmic imprints accumulated over lifetimes (samskaras).Therefore, path of yoga is the surest, subtlest, quickest and most effective method to attain liberation. Yoga practices, done with utmost intensity and mindfulness, work in the subtle and gross bodies to effectively bring down the tendencies and destroy all the samskaras that works as the cause of rebirth. The soul, thus, on its own volition, leaves its physical form, merges with the eternal cosmic energy, and achieves liberation from the cycle of reincarnation. This is the highest state of yoga. Even with dedicated adherence to the prescribed path, a yogi's practices do not guarantee the attainment of ultimate liberation (yogamukti) within their current lifetime. This situation could be due to his samskaras from past lives or ineffectiveness of the practices that he follows now. However, the effort he put in will ultimately bear fruit. Every effort made on the spiritual path is believed to create positive karmic imprints (samskaras), which accumulate across lifetimes, ultimately ensuring continued evolution and progress toward spiritual realization in future existences. The instinctive imprints (samskaras) formed will help him to continue the yogic practices and will help him to complete the journey. Therefore, the path of Yoga offers a wealth of benefits. While the various paths of yoga, such as Raja yoga, Tantra yoga, Kundalini yoga, Mantra yoga, Laya yoga, Siddha yoga, Kriya yoga, and Hatha yoga feature diverse practices, they ultimately share the same supreme goal and destination.

Some individuals of great spiritual stature experience enlightenment spontaneously, or through non-traditional paths, rather than through structured yoga practices. All their inherent yogic powers will awaken naturally. They attain sainthood without any real effort. The accumulated spiritual momentum made in previous existences get carry forward, allowing one to finish their spiritual journey and achieve enlightenment in this lifetime.

Pursuing the path of devotion(Bhakti Marg), can lead one to spiritual liberation (moksha) and the achievement of union with the divine (yoga). When a devotee fully surrenders, their ego gets sublimated, allowing them to achieve their ultimate spiritual goal. Poonthanam, Saint Kabir, and Meera were all prominent figures in the Bhakti movement who devoted their lives to intense spiritual practice and achieving mergence or union with God. The person can submit himself to any deity he chooses, such as Lord Shiva, Lord Krishna, Kali or Devi. Immersing oneself in unwavering devotion and faith for a chosen deity can lead to the sublimation of the worshiper's ego and facilitate a spiritual awakening. Whatever can be attained through the discipline of yogic practices can also be achieved through the path of unwavering devotion. A mind that continuously focuses on the remembrance of divinity achieves the weakening of samskaras (latent impressions), naturally diverting attention from distractions and facilitating the attainment of yoga siddhi (perfection or success in yoga). Just as a yogi, through the continuous discipline and dedication, characteristic of a warrior, achieves the state of yoga, so too does a worshiper achieve the same profound state through the unwavering path of devotion. So, Bhakti Yoga can be summed up as the spiritual practice centered on devotion and love for a personal God or deity. Though the paths differ, the destination remains the same. The only difference is that each person follows the path best suited to their individual nature.

Many people achieve this state by following the path of action, or karma yoga. For them, the action itself is its own reward and the highest goal. A person who performs actions without attachment to the results, viewing themselves as an instrument of divine will, with a God-centered perspective where all actions and outcomes are seen as divine intention, embodies the principles of Karma Yoga and can be referred to as a Karma yogi. Individuals with ego-less action also achieve perfect spiritual union (yoga siddhi) by eliminating their karmic impressions (samskaras).

A different group is dedicated to the acquisition of knowledge. They question themselves with profound and mysterious queries: 'Who am I? Where did all these beings originate? Where are they traveling through the cycle of births and deaths? What is the cause of the genesis of the eternal universe?' In their unending quest for wisdom, they dissect each answer, considering every possible angle and implication.

Resorting to any of the paths—bhakti, yoga, or karma—leads to the stillness of mind. Regulating the mind is the foundational first step for any endeavor, and that focused state of awareness is precisely what is cultivated through the practice of meditation (dhyana). When you concentrate intensely on a single subject, your attention naturally shifts away from other matters. This singular focus causes the general thought process to slow down. If maintained over time, the overall flow of thoughts gradually diminishes and eventually stops. To regulate the mind and end the thought process, different paths resort to different methods; that is the core difference. In the path of Yoga, the soul serves as the focal point, while in the path of devotion, God is the object of focus. For those following the path of Jnana Marga, intellect takes center stage, and in Karma Yoga, action is emphasized. Integrating medicinal applications to achieve the goals of yoga is a common practice. Man, in his pursuit of reality, has found ways to harness energy from the sleeping state. Through the use of distinctive and powerful herbs, the mind is calmed and the ten life-giving forces (dasha pranas) are brought into balance; like yogis calm their mind through yogic practices. Shri Nagarjuna the Jaina Theerthankaras are believed to have attained a high yogic state through the use of medicinal applications.

What is Enlightenment?

Enlightenment is the ultimate goal towards which all individuals strive, regardless of the path they follow, be it yoga, devotion, or selfless action (karma); many roads, one destination. It is expressed in different terms as salvation, liberation, Samadhi, final emancipation (Kaivalyam), Supreme state (paramapadam) etc.

The state of enlightenment can be explained in several distinct ways: from a scientific perspective, it can be understood neurologically through the lens of modern neuroscience; through the framework of modern psychological theories; and, in accordance with the principles of yoga, as a journey of feelings, experiences, and spiritual progress.

Enlightenment from a yogic philosophical perspective

In the Yoga Sutras, Sage Patanjali defines yoga as the cessation of mental activity through consistent practice, a process aimed at dissolving false identities and achieving enlightenment. The core principle is that enlightenment occurs when the mind's actions and fluctuations are completely stilled. This constant and continuous discipline leads to the removal of the mind's impositions, revealing one's true nature.

While 'mind' is widely recognized as a noun, referring to the faculty of consciousness, it functions as a verb. Except during deep sleep, the mind is constantly active. While we are conscious, countless thoughts stream through the brain. A thought originates in a deeper part of the mind, develops, and surfaces to our awareness. As one thought fades, another emerges. When you examine the mind, you will find that a continuous and incessant flow of thoughts persists at all times, the only exception being when you are in a deep state of sleep. Thoughts continue till before falling asleep, just before waking up, and while in a half-asleep or drowsy state. In a wakeful state, thoughts manifest as language or inner speech, while in a dream state, they take the form of images and sensory experiences. In yogic philosophies, the ultimate goal, often referred to as moksha (liberation) or kaivalya (emancipation), is complete cessation of all thoughts; a state of profound stillness and control over the mind's constant fluctuations (vrittis). 'Chitta Vritti nirodha' refers to the regulation and eventual stilling of the mind's thought processes. It involves slowing down the constant flow of choice-making and achieving freedom from the mind's ideational choices until the mental activity naturally ceases.

According to Yoga shastra, mind has four conditions: Alertness (jagrath), dream (swapna), deep sleep (sushupthi), Thureeyam -fourth stage in the cycle of births and deaths – individual soul merging with the Universal soul. 'Jagrath' refers to the waking state, the condition in which the mind is aware of the external world and identifies with the ego, or individual self. We also have some emerging thoughts. Therefore, we can understand that the state of jagrath (alertness) encompasses the presence of thoughts concurrent with the awareness of those thoughts. In this state, there is both the activity of the mind and a conscious recognition of that mental activity. When dreaming, awareness is absent due to the state of sleep; dreams are simply thoughts that manifest during this slumber state. At that stage, there is only unconsciousness; thoughtless unawareness. In a state of perfect, dreamless sleep, our experience is one of pure unconsciousness, devoid of thoughts or mental activity. This stage of slumber is characterized by a profound, thoughtless absence of awareness. The ultimate goal of yoga is to attain Turiya, often referred to as the "fourth state". This state transcends the ordinary states of consciousness: wakefulness (jagrat), dreaming (swapna), and deep sleep (sushupti). In Turiya, the individual soul (jivatma) merges with the universal soul (paramatma), signifying a state of pure consciousness, absolute reality, and profound union. It is the wakeful state where we have complete awareness, void of thoughts. That is, pure consciousness (Thureeyam). This itself is Bhramapadam – state of ultimate bliss, God realization and liberation. This state, known also as Samadhi, represents a state of meditative absorption, describes a profound merging with the supreme reality. Pure consciousness is blissful, devoid of disturbance or vexation - ultimate blissful state. It is the state of complete freedom. Every spiritual practitioner attempts to achieve this state of complete freedom.

Jagrath - pure consciousness + thoughts
Dream state – unconsciousness/unawareness + thoughts
Deep sleep – unconsciousness/unawareness + thoughts
Thureeyam - pure consciousness with no thoughts

Pure consciousness is akin to an ocean; deep and infinite.

Thoughts/mind is the waves (vibrations) that arise in the shore of the great ocean. Thoughts are transient turbulence that appear near the edge of our awareness, while a profound stillness resides in the depths of consciousness itself. While the shores are subject to the constant, turbulent crash of waves, the ocean depths remain in perpetual quietude. Consciousness is the fundamental reality, much like the ocean is the basis for all waves; thoughts (waves) are transient expressions of the deeper, enduring ocean of consciousness, which remains even when thoughts cease. Thoughts are like fleeting clouds against the eternal backdrop of the sky; the sky represents the enduring nature of consciousness, which remains even as thoughts come and go. Like the clouds appear and disappear in the sky, thoughts also appear and disappear in the vastness of consciousness. The state of Kaivalya, described in the Yoga Sutras, is one of absolute pure consciousness; often compared to the expansive stillness of a cloudless sky. The text suggests that individuals can attain this enlightened state through persistent, systematic, and continuous spiritual practices.

A state of profound bliss, inherent to our existence, emerges when the mind achieves perfect stillness and the purity of consciousness is realized. This internal stillness allows one to access an eternal and naturally occurring state of inner peace and happiness. Acceleration in the speed and volume of thoughts intensifies mental restlessness, resulting in significant mental and physical agitation. When experiencing calmness and observing the mind, one notices that the rate and rapidity of thoughts are significantly reduced. The mind achieves a state where thoughts are fewer and farther between. The more one thinks, the more unhappy and sorrowful one becomes; conversely, decreasing one's thoughts leads to greater bliss and happiness. The pursuit of a "thoughtless state" referred to as Samadhi is a central concept in spiritual traditions, which describe it as the ultimate state of existence where all mental distractions cease. Considered as the goal of spiritual journey, everyone keeps looking for this blissful state only. However, our inability to regulate our minds, due to a lack of acquired techniques, prevents us from achieving that state, resulting in increased distress. Patanjali's Yogasutras delineates a comprehensive system, primarily the eight limbs of yoga (Ashtanga Yoga), as the instruments or path to attain the blissful state of Samadhi or liberation. It explains how one can go beyond the mind and reach the blissful state of Self awareness by systematic practice. The permanent and lasting state of spiritual knowledge, typically accessible to a dedicated Yogi, is an experience everyone has likely encountered at least temporarily at some point in their lives. During the most intense moment of sexual union, an individual may reach a peak experience characterized by a cessation of thought and a profound stillness of mind. This ecstatic state represents the highest degree of happiness achievable in that specific moment; however, it is inherently transient. A Yogi continuously experiences this blissful state, dwelling in it permanently. This individual is one who has attained the realization of God.

Spiritual Enlightenment (Awakening) based on Nervous System

The central nervous system is primarily composed of the brain and the spinal cord. The brain includes the cerebrum, which is made up of billions of neurons. The central nervous system works in conjunction with the peripheral nervous system, which includes all the nerves that branch out from the brain to reach the rest of the body. Endocrine glands such as the liver, pituitary gland and the pineal gland, which produce hormones, are also part of the Central Nervous system. This Central Nervous System is instrumental in controlling physical and mental activities of human being. The cerebrum or brain is the centre of all activities. The nerves that originate from the cerebrum passes through the neck and goes down up to the tips of each fingers in both the legs. The Bhagavad Gita uses the metaphor of an “upside-down tree” where the primary source, or “root” is at the top (referring to the crown of the head or the ultimate reality), and the intricate network of the nervous system, like “branches” spreads downward throughout the body. It is solely through the nervous system that individuals develop self-awareness and the capacity to perceive and react to external environment.

It demonstrates the critical role of the central nervous system in the existence of a being. A common scientific perspective holds that human beings possess the most complex and developed nervous system among all species, which facilitates them to have special divine power than other beings.

According to ancient Indian philosophy and spiritual texts, the body's control is managed by an intricate network of 72,000 'nadis' (energy channels) that emanate from a central point near the cerebrum and extend throughout the entire physical and subtle body, influencing both physiological and psychological processes. The three most significant channels, out of many, are known as the Ida, Pingala, and Sushumna nadis. They emerge from the cerebrum; pass through the spine to the tips of the finger of both the legs. Nerve Ida originates from the tip of right big toe, travels through the left hand side of the spine and stops at the back of the right eye. Having a cooling, lunar nature, it cools down the body. Also, nerve Ida is connected to the left nostril. When one breathes through the left nostril, it can be assumed that the energy (prana) is flowing through nerve Ida. Nerve Pingala starts from the left big toe spreads up to the back of left eye. Its property is heat in nature. It increases heat in the body. It is stated in some of the texts that Ida and Pingala end in the left and right nostrils respectively. These nerves located in the sides of spine are termed according to their attributes as Chandra nadi (Ida) and soorya nadi (Pingala). Spinal cord (central energy channel) is situated in the centre of the body originating from the Brahmarandra (an aperture on top of the head – in new born child this part will be very soft), gets down through spinal cord and reaches Mooladharam situated between the anus and sexual organs. The Sushumna Nadi is considered the crucial pathway for the flow of vital energy (prana) that, when activated and balanced, leads to the state of enlightenment.This channel is described as being temperate in nature, symbolizing a state of equilibrium.

The intricate network of the body's nerve cells, known as the nervous system, serves as a crucial communication highway. It is responsible for transmitting the sensory input gathered through our five senses up to the cerebrum. Conversely, this very system also relays signals and instructions originating in the brain to various parts of the body, thereby coordinating and sustaining their activity. The nervous system is essential for coordinating all human activities, both internal and external. It acts as the body's control center, through which vital energy (bio-electric current) flows, much like electrical current through a house's wiring. This flow allows organs and limbs to function, sustaining life and enabling movement and thought.

Energy (Prana) flow through the Spinal cord (Brahma naadi)

It has already been mentioned that the central energetic channel is referred to as the Sushumna Nadi (or sushumna), which is situated inside the spine, flanked by the Ida and Pingala nadis. Breathing is a continuous, automatic process that occurs whether an individual is awake or asleep. The cessation of breathing halts the bodily systems responsible for generating and distributing energy, at which point an individual is pronounced dead. We draw in vital energy -oxygen- through our nostrils, a process essential for survival and powering various bodily functions. The air we inhale, rich in oxygen, is the "life force" our bodies need to operate effectively. Various gaseous waste products are expelled through the nostrils as well.

When you pay close attention to the continuous process of breathing, you will notice that at any given moment, air flows more freely through one of your nostrils than the other. This phenomenon is a natural physiological cycle in the body. Gently block one nostril with your finger and breathe through the other; the nostril that feels more open and allows easier airflow shows where your "life force" (prana) flows more freely. When the left nostril is dominant, the Ida nerve (nadi) is considered more active and influential. Conversely, when the right nostril is more open, the Pingala nerve is thought to be effective and efficient.

This keeps on changing every hour. If the life force flows through Ida nerve for one hour, it will change to Pingala nerve, for next hour. According to yogic principles, there is a brief period when both the ida (left) and pingala (right) energy channels (nadis) are concurrently active, allowing the central energy channel (sushumna) within the spinal cord to awaken for approximately four minutes. At this time, energy flows to both parts – left and right – evenly, in a uniform manner. This is the principle of balanced state (Samadhi). When Ida nerve is active, the right part of the cerebrum will be energized. Similarly, when the Pingala nerve is active, the left side of the cerebrum will function effectively. The state of Samadhi (sama + dhee) is achieved when both cerebral hemispheres operate in a balanced manner, resulting in a state of deep absorption. Dhee means intellect (Bhudhi). When the Samadhi state is achieved, prana flows continuously through the spinal cord, leading one to reach lofty heights of spirituality. While a normal person experiences a specific flow or activation of energy every hour, a yogi, through advanced practices like pranayama, mudras, bandhas, and other esoteric techniques, attains and continuously maintains this energetic state within the spinal cord. In this condition, both the nostrils will be in an open state. One who achieves this state will experience a divine transformation, reaching the exalted condition of a yogi and attaining sainthood, ultimately becoming a Siddha. They will perceive an inner divine radiance, become omniscient, and transcend the limitations of time and space. Throughout time immemorial, the state of everlasting life has served as the ultimate aim of spiritual pursuit.

The Triveni Sangam, the sacred confluence witnessed during the Kumbh Mela, is considered the external physical manifestation of the internal spiritual anatomy. In this symbolism, the Yamuna River represents Ida, the Ganges represents Pingala, and the mythical Saraswati River embodies the central energy channel, the spinal cord (sushumna).

Kundalini Yoga: The Path to Enlightenment

Kundalini yoga describes that a vast, unlimited energy is believed to lie dormant at the base of the spine, the navel region. Through specific yogic practices, this concealed energy is awakened and guided upward along the spinal cord. The energy passes through "rings situated in the spine" and ultimately arrive at the "Sahasra Dala Padmam" (thousand-petaled lotus).This journey through the various energy centers is associated with a wide range of profound spiritual and mystical experiences for the practitioner. He also experiences mental and spiritual elevations. Kundalini Yoga explains that the ultimate spiritual awakening is achieved when the practitioner's energy ascends past the Ajna chakra and reaches the Sahasrara chakra (Sahasra dala padma).This journey culminates in Brahmapadam, a state of profound spiritual enlightenment that represents the ultimate goal of spiritual practice.

The practitioner will have to practice many kriyas in order to achieve this state. Kundalini Yoga is presented as a spiritual discipline aimed at achieving the awareness of the Divine (Brahmanjanam) within one's current lifetime, under the guidance of a Guru. This path involves specific practices, including Pranayama (breathing exercises),

Mudras (hand gestures or body postures), Bandhas (energy locks), and combinations thereof, to facilitate this ultimate spiritual awakening. Awakening the potent energy of Kundalini is considered an advanced practice that requires extreme precision and care.Guiding this powerful force along its intended path to the Sahasrara is a hazardous endeavor, necessitating rigorous discipline and, often, expert supervision. Following incorrect practices, even in minor instances, can lead to serious consequences such as mental depression, lethargy, indifference, body temperature variations, skin diseases, impeded personal growth, and sleep deprivation. If the awakened Kundalini energy deviates from the proper central channel, it risks becoming stuck in a chakra or following an incorrect path through other nerves, which could adversely affect physical functions in the organs and limbs. To redirect to the correct path is an arduous task; therefore, those pursuing this field are advised to learn these techniques from an adept Guru. It is inaccurate to claim that Kundalini yoga is a component of the Ashtanga yoga system as described by Sage Patanjali; the two are distinct yoga traditions with different philosophical foundations and practices. Patanjali's Yoga Sutras delineate an eight-limbed path to samadhi (Ashtanga: Yama, Niyama, Asana, Pranayama, Pratyahara, Dharana, Dhyana, Samadhi), whereas Kundalini yoga is a separate spiritual discipline focusing on the awakening of dormant energy at the base of the spine. It is observed that some pranayama methods and mudras are common across all yogic paths. However, there are also unique kriyas practiced exclusively in Kundalini Yoga. In Hatha Yoga, there are numerous postures (asanas) designed for physical training, while Ashtanga Yoga employs a more limited set of techniques focused on achieving physical well-being. The core practices of yoga-which include Pranayama (breath control), Dhyanam (meditation), Dharana (steadfast focus), and Samadhi (a balanced state)-share fundamental training methodologies. The primary differences lie in the specific application of the practices, varying in the quantity and quality of kriyas (cleansing techniques) and mudras (symbolic gestures/seals) utilized within each discipline. It has been observed that many practitioners blend methods from various streams of yoga. In pursuit of the same objective, seekers often study under different teachers and experiment with a variety of prescribed techniques to discover the approach most suited to their individual needs. This eclectic approach is a primary source of the perceived confusion. Through this mutual exchange of ideas and techniques, yogic methods are continuously refined and their efficacy enhanced, facilitating their spread across the globe.

The Power of Kundalini

The fundamental basis of all living beings is the continuous flow of life force, often conceptualized as bio-electrical current or vital energy. This energy flow is essential for every biological activity and expression of life. Existence ceases the instant this flow of energy stops. Therefore, the body sustains this vital energy through two primary mechanisms: the intake of food (metabolism) and the reception of power from the Universal source (a broader, potentially spiritual, energy). Continuous use of the body's energy reserves depletes them, leading to a feeling of fatigue. Vitality is restored through replenishment, specifically by getting adequate rest and consuming nutritious foods. This cycle of energy depletion and replenishment is a fundamental process that continues throughout one's lifetime.

Kundalini yoga suggests that humans possess a source of unlimited, dormant power, akin to atomic energy, which exists in addition to the standard bio-energy needed for daily activities. This potent, inactive energy is situated in the Mulaadhara (root chakra) - an oval-shaped area located below the navel, between the anus and the sexual organs. Kundalini is a powerful, latent energy often visualized as a coiled serpent resting at the base of the spine. This energy is symbolically described as being dormant in a bowl or cave-like space, where the spinal cord originates. It remains in a sleeping state, with its head pointing downwards, until awakened.

When viewed through the lens of modern nervous system theories, this can be understood in a different manner. The Sushumna nadi, which is the central subtle energy channel originates from the brain, moves through the middle of vertebrae in the spine and goes down through the coccyx (tail bone) which is in a triangular shape. It then branches out, with the terminal points reaching the reproductive organs. The tips of certain nerves form in a shell-shaped area located below the navel, which is why the concept of the Kundalini power is traditionally described as being latent or dormant in that specific region. When a Kundalini practitioner through yoga practices activate/stimulate this energy, it gets out of slumber and moves to the top of the Sushmna nerve and breaks through every energy centers, reaches the Sahasrara. He acquires super natural powers and attains eternal bliss; the state of realizing God/Super soul. It is also interpreted as the Union of Shivasakthi (Union of Shiva, principle of divine consciousness and Shakti, principle of divine energy). The practitioner at this stage loses sense of duality and shines as the embodiment of Existence, Consciousness, and Bliss –Sat-chit-Ananda swaroopam. This blissful state of Self-realization(liberation) is sought by millions of seekers and only a few blessed souls attain this state.

For practitioners of various yogic disciplines such as Pranayama, Hatha yoga, and Kundalini yoga, the opening of the Sushumna nadi and the subsequent rush of energy can be an immediate and palpable experience, often described as a sudden vibration. This direct, personal experience fosters a steadfast faith in the existence and power of Kundalini energy and the associated energy centers, or chakras. However, in those who follow Hamsa vidhya (a profound spiritual teaching or practice, particularly in the context of Yoga and Vedanta philosophy), Sidha vidhya(supreme knowledge of yogic attainment), vasee yoga (mastery of breathing and control over one's senses actions) etc., opening of Sushmna nerve and flow of energy up to Sahasrara will be natural and gentle and they will not experience vibration of any kind. Therefore, they do not accept or recognize Kundalini power or energy centers.

Chakaras or six Spiritual Centers (Shada-Adharas)

The term chakra is central to Yogic science and spiritual practices focused on facilitating human spiritual ascension, with a particular emphasis in the discipline of Kundalini Yoga. These are the locations in a body where the Kundalini power or life force reaches in different stages, yet their presence is not perceptible to the senses. It is situated in the energy fields of subtle body. The food sheath, or Annamaya kosha, is the physical, perceptible layer of the self. It is the most tangible of the five koshas. In contrast, the Pranamaya kosha, or energy sheath is subtle and not directly visible to the physical eye. While unseen, its existence can be distinctly felt through an awareness of the body's vital life force, such as through breathing, yoga practices, and a general sense of vitality or energy flow.The Pranamayakosha, the energy sheath, permeates and completely fill the Annamayakosha. Within that framework are five distinct sheaths: the Mind sheath (Manomayakosha), the Intellect/Knowledge sheath (Vijnanamayakosha), and others. The Pranamaya Kosha, the vital energy sheath, is comprised of five main life-force currents known as the Pancha Pranas: Prana Vayu (inward flow, intake), Apana Vayu (downward/outward flow), Samana Vayu (assimilation, digestion), Udana Vayu (upward flow) and Vyana Vayu (circulation, pervading the entire body); working together to animate the physical and subtle body. Pranamaya Kosha is the level of subtle energy flow that keeps the intellect, mind and the limbs of body active. Chakras are primarily associated with the Pranamaya Kosha, which governs the flow of prana or life force through the nadis. The energy flow in the body is running along the spine, with the various chakras serving as a series of connected energy centers located at specific points along this central channel.

We can alternatively conceptualize the chakras in this way: Building on the understanding that sensory inputs from the five senses travel to the brain for processing, the subsequent instructions sent by the brain to the various parts of the body are transmitted via the nervous system. The Sushumna nerve, described as residing within the central canal of the spine, is understood to descend and branch out, innervating the left and right sides of the body all the way to the fingertips of the feet. The most important of these nerves are the Sushumna, Ida and Pingala. We have learned about the nature and orientation of the Ida and Pingala energy pathways. In spiritual traditions and also all over the world, the central rod and the two entwined snakes of symbols resembling the Caduceus are indeed interpreted as representations of the body's primary energy channels (Sushumna, the central channel (the rod) Ida and Pingala, the left and right channels (the two snakes) that spiral around Sushumna). The area where the snakes are entwined are called chakras oraadharas. It functions similarly to power distribution substations, breaking down and directing the main supply. These points can also be seen as connections between major endocrine and vital organs-specifically the reproductive glands, pancreas, thymus gland, kidneys, liver, heart, thyroid, pituitary gland, and pineal gland-all of which regulate bodily functions. Chakras are sometimes conceptualized as the energy layers surrounding the central axis of the body, much like the concentric layers found within a hollow bamboo stalk.

In Yogic philosophy, the concept is that the body's subtle energy system (not the physical nervous system) contains 72,000 channels called nadis that distribute vital life-force energy, or prana. These nadis converge at specific energy centers known as chakras, which are considered main junctions. Moolaadhara, Swadhishtanam, Manipoorakam, Anaahatham, Vishuddhi, Anjna are those main chakras. The Sahasrara, often described as the crown chakra, is viewed as transcending all others. It is conceptually linked to the function and location of the physical brain. While certain texts describe additional chakras beyond the Sahasrara, the foundational system

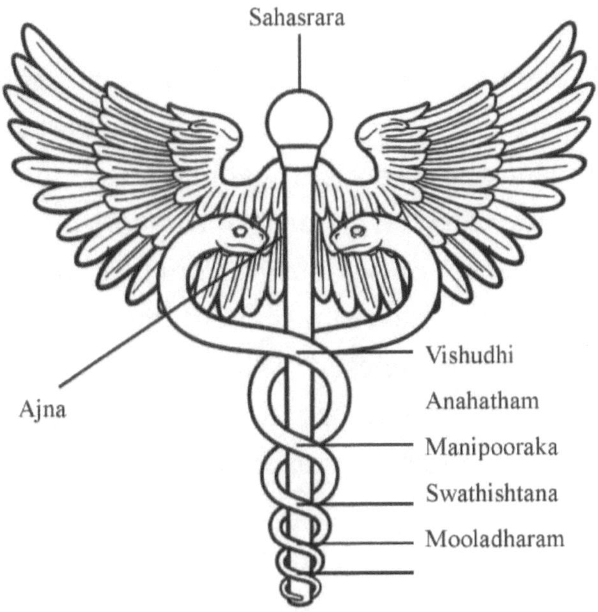

widely embraced by most yoga practitioners centers on the

traditional Shadadharas (the six lower chakras) and the thousand-petaled lotus, or Sahasra-dala-padma.

Reaching the Goal after crossing over the six steps (Realization of God after breaking through the Shad chakras)

When you cross the six steps and reach there, you will see Lord Shiva" is a bhajan line that holds profound spiritual significance within Hindu tradition, often interpreted as an allegory for the devotee's journey through different stages of spiritual evolution to attain divine consciousness. The "six steps" metaphorically represent the transcendence of various material or psychological states, leading to the realization of the ultimate reality (Lord Shiva) within oneself. When the dormant feminine life force, often referred to as Kundalini, is awakened through spiritual practice, it ascends through the six energy centers known as the shadadharas (chakras). Upon reaching the Sahasrara chakra at the crown of the head, it merges with Shiva, the masculine energy principle. This union of energies is believed to lead the practitioner to an experience of profound, ineffable bliss and enlightenment. In yogic philosophies, the Mooladhara is conceptualized as the negative pole, and the Sahasrara is seen as the positive pole.The movement of energy along the subtle channels of the body (Nadis) between these two points is believed by practitioners to activate specific physiological centers, such as the penile gland, and lead to an experience of profound spiritual bliss.

Moolaadhaaram – The root Chakra

It is located at the base of the spine, in the perineum area between the anus and the genitals. In coccyx, the tail bone- last of the spinal column, is where it is positioned. In the bottom of coccyx which is in triangular shape, there is a microscopic opening through which Sushmna nerve comes out and spreads as branches to the reproductive organs. To be specific, this microscopic opening is the centre of Mooladhara - Sanskrit words "moola" (root) and "adhara" (seat). Kundalini power is latent here. It is the base of self knowledge and the grounding principle of spiritual journey. When it is awakened, the practitioner starts to get a taste of knowledge. He can now overcome fear. Body becomes lighter.

This chakra has four petals, symbolizing Manas, Bhudhi, Chitha and Ahankara. It is red in colour. Each chakra has been described as lotuses having various, distinct number of petals. It is depicted as cluster of nerves that spreads to various parts of body from the respective parts of the spine, situated in and around spine. In nutshell, four branches of nerves spread to various parts of the body, from Moolaadhara. The Beej manathra (condensed, potent sounds that can directly activate energy centers) is "LAM."

Mooladhara chakra has petals having Beej manthras "VAM", SHAM", " śaṃ", "SAM." The vibrations that are created when these beej manthras are recited, reverberates and stimulates the chain of nerves. This will be discussed in depth in the portion " Manthra Sadhana." Mooladhara chakra is linked to earth element, one of the five elements.

Swadhishtana

Swadhishtana Chakra is situated above Mooladhara, vermilion in colour, having six petals, represents water element. Beeja manthra is "VAM." The Beeja manthra of six petals are "BAM", "BHAM", "MAM", "YAM". "RAM", "LAM". Sexual organs are the location of Swadhishtana Chakra.

When this chakra is energized, a practitioner may experience enhanced proficiency in literacy, arts, and crafts, along with the awakening of spiritual wisdom and the revelation of hidden knowledge. The activation of this energy center is associated with a surge in creative and intellectual capabilities, as well as profound spiritual insight. When this chakra is activated, it leads to the removal of ignorance, a manifestation of spiritual awakening, and the emergence of new perceptions. The Swadhisthana chakra is considered paramount among the chakras. It is located about two inches below the navel area. This area is regarded as the center of the body's life energy, a belief supported by the concentration of numerous nerves in this region. When a yoga practitioner uses various pranayama methods to awaken the internal fire (known as agni) in the navel area, the resulting energy expansion and pressure stimulate both the Swadhisthana and Manipura chakras. When energy flows and strengthens through the specific nerve associated with the Svadhisthana chakra, the practitioner can experience the resulting vibrations. While the Mooladhara chakra is described as the dwelling place of Kundalini energy, the core assertion is that the process of awakening the Swadhisthana Chakra (sacral chakra) stimulates and "opens" the nerves of the lower region, leading practitioners to experience intense vibrations. When the naval area is activated by the heat generated from pranayama practice, the practitioner may feel a sensation akin to a small serpent descending towards the Mooladhara chakra. This signifies that the dormant Kundalini energy has been aroused and begins its upward journey, aiming to enter the Sushumna Nadi from the Swadhisthana chakra. (Illustration-2)

When in the mother's womb, all the nutrients essential for physical and mental development are transported to the baby via the umbilical cord, the attachment point of which later forms the navel area. Therefore it is the most important centre connected to our existence. In Japanese culture, particularly within the context of the historical practice of harakiri, the abdominal area held significant cultural and symbolic importance. It was often considered the "seat of life" or the soul. The act itself was a ritualistic form of suicide performed by samurai and other high-ranking individuals to regain or preserve honour.

Manipooraka Chakra

The Manipura Chakra, or solar plexus, is a vital energy center located just above the navel. Often described as the body's "powerhouse," it is associated with the element of fire and a yellow colour. This chakra is considered crucial for fostering willpower and establishing a strong sense of purpose. This chakra has ten petals and Beeja manthra is "RAM." This chakra, with the petals having beeja manthras "DAM", "DDAM", THAM", "DHAM", "DAM", "PAM", "FAM" is activated, the physical power and the vibrancy of the practitioner reaches new spiritual heights. Vitality (subtle life force) increases and divine glow (effulgence like radiance) manifests in the body. He will no longer be afraid of fire, will be relieved of all kinds of diseases. Since this chakra is connected to the digestive system, this is the source of energy for all physical activities. When the power of Kundalini reaches this chakra, the practitioner experiences spiritual awakening. The area from Moolaadhara to below the Manipooraka is known as Sooryamandala and the area from Manipooraka to just below Vishuddhi is called Agni mandala. The regions above Vishudhi, including head is known as Chandara mandala. The energy generated by the Kundalini is hot in nature from the Muladhara chakra up to the Vishuddhi chakra, and becomes cool or cold in nature from the Vishuddhi and above (Anahata, Ajna, Sahasrara).

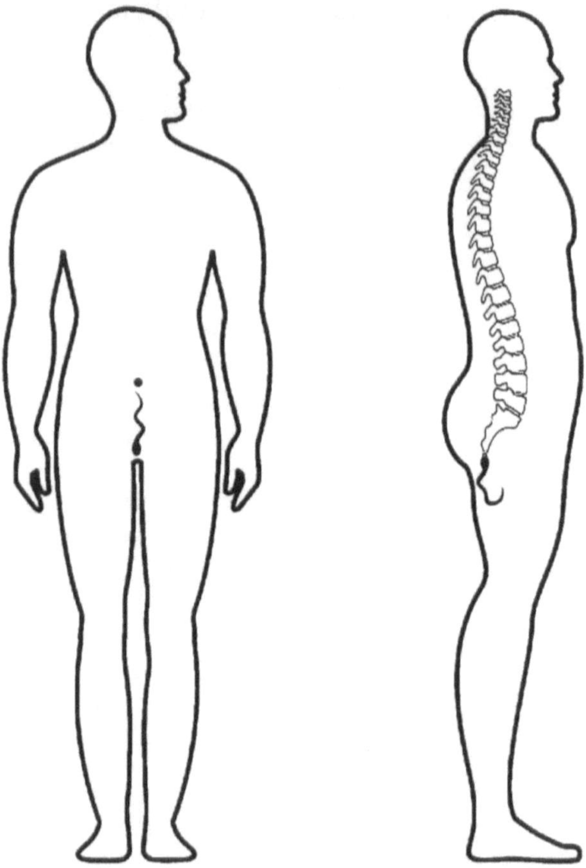

Kundalini gets awakened from the naval area and moves downwards | After breaking through Moolaadhara Chakra, Kundalini enters Sushmna.

Illustration 2

Anaahatham

Anahata Chakra, also known as the Heart Chakra, is metaphorically associated with the heart center of the body's energy system. This central location signifies its role in love, compassion, and emotional balance. colour green/ rising sun. Beeja manthra, "YAM". It is with twelve petals, Beejaksharas being "KAM", 'KHAM", "GAM", "GHAM", "NAM", "CHAM", "CHHAM", "JAM", "LSAM", "NJAM", "TAM", "DDAM". Anahatha chakram has Air as its element. When the Anahatha Chakra is awakened, the practitioner will have complete control over wind principle (Vayuthatva). The word Anahata signifies a state of pristine Consciousness and spiritual freshness that remains "unhurt" or "unstuck" by the dualities and emotional turmoil of the material world. By controlling the movement of life force by one's own will power, the practitioner gets complete mastery over the sense organs. Chakras below the Anahatha are all related to spiritual powers that are body centered. Since the Anahatha Chakra is related to the working of the mind and its fluctuation, this chakra has a prominent position in Spirituality. When the Anahata (heart) chakra is activated by the awakened Kundalini power, the yogi attains a state of profound compassion and unconditional love. They become a source and channel for this supernatural love, living in harmony and deep attunement with nature. This phase of spiritual awakening allows the individual to embody universal love as their primary state of being.

Vishudhi Chakra

Vishudhi Chakra (the purification centre) represents the space (Aaksash) element, Beeja manathram, "HAM". This chakra has sixteen petals and the beeja mantra of the petals are "AM", "AAM", "IM", "EEM", "UM","OOM", "RUM", "ROOM", "LRUM", "LROOM", "AYAM", "AAYAM", "OHM", "OUM", "ANG", "Ah". Representation colour gray/blue and is considered as the center of spiritual purification. It is connected with hearing/ear, among the five sense organs. The Vishuddhi Chakra, often referred to as the "throat chakra," plays a vital role in spiritual practice and is located in the throat region. Through dedicated practice, an individual can direct their Kundalini energy upwards to this specific energy center. A significant milestone in this path is the "breaking through" of the Vishuddhi Chakra, after which the Kundalini power is said to naturally find its own upward path through the remaining chakras. The practitioner has a limited role in this matter.The pranic energy is absolutely purified at this stage, that is why it is called Vishudhi chakra. To safeguard the cosmos from annihilation by the Kalakooda poison, Lord Shiva absorbed it into his being, holding it in his throat where it turned blue; a profound act of sacrifice that made him Neelakanta, the protector of the universe. Only when it moves down, it will be really be poisonous. May be, this could be a mythological narration/illustration of pranic energy attaining purity when it reaches this chakra.

The nature of Kundalini energy up to Vishudhi Chakra is hot and above Vishudhi, it is cold. Moreover, when this energy reaches in every other chakra, the practitioner will experience a pleasant state of coolness accompanied by serenity. As energy passes through any chakra located below the Vishuddhi chakra, that area feels intensely hot; subsequently, as the energy moves on, a sensation of coolness takes its place. Conversely, in all chakras above the Vishuddhi, the sensation experienced is exclusively one of coolness.

When Kundalini energy reaches Vishudhi Chakra, the practitioner gains exceptional oratorial skill. Voice tone becomes crystal clear. Effortless oratory skill and aptitude in music will Manifest. He will have complete control over his voice and will show command over delivery of speech. The person's statements will be exceptionally insightful and irrefutable due to a vast well of knowledge and the acquisition of scientific understanding. Additionally, they will possess the extraordinary ability of clairaudience, or extra-sensory hearing.

Ajna Chakra (Third-eye Chakra)

Ajna Chakra is positioned in the centre of eyebrows, just at the beginning of nose. Representing colour, Indigo. It is the position of Third-eye which is the seat of transcendental/Super sensuous knowledge. The ascent/progress of Kundalini power - that was purified at Vishudhi Chakra - to Ajna Chakra and then to Sahasraara is phenomenal. The life force, having moved through the chakras one by one, now takes a sudden leap from the Vishuddha (throat center) to the higher energy centers.

Spiritual powers and heightened intuition may begin to manifest in a practitioner as energy approaches the Ajna Chakra, often referred to as the "third eye" or the center of intuition. With eyes closed, he can perceive the cosmic knowledge through the Third eye. This chakra, is believed to grant individuals profound spiritual insights and intuitive abilities. It is not limited to understanding distant cosmic phenomena but also enables the perception of subtle energetic and psychological shifts within oneself and others. Even without modern tools, ancient sages of Bharatha gained profound, exact knowledge of the cosmos through deep inner vision, meditation, and spiritual insight, accessing universal truths directly from consciousness rather than external observation. They used focused inner exploration, contemplation, and inquiry to understand both the inner self and the outer universe, revealing profound realities through direct experience.

The Beeja Manthra of Anjna Chakra is 'OHM" and has two petals having "HAM"and "KSHAM" as Beeja Manthra. In human body, it is connected to the pituitary gland. When it is awakened, one will have knowledge about mysterious and secretive subjects and he will become Omniscient. By concentrating on the Third-eye he will get to know about any subject; on his own. He will also know how to transmigrate the soul into another body. He can focus easily on Shambhaavi Mudra and Unmini (state of thoughtlessness) very easily. Thereafter, Yogi can continue on deep meditation without any kind of disturbances and unsteadiness.

SAHASRAARA, the Crown Chakra

Sahasrara is known as the 'thousand petalled lotus. Since ' thousand' is used to denote many or innumerable number, we can say, it has countless petals. Violet colour. Kundalini power that breaches Ajna Chakara and reaches Sahasrara, merges with Shiva Shakthi and the yogi spiritually becomes 'Sat-cit-ānanda. This state, the pinnacle of spirituality, is also described as a path to Yoga, Liberation, Samadhi, Knowledge of Brahman (Self-Realization), Salvation or Enlightenment. When all the nerve cells in the brain are energized, the practitioner experiences the blossoming of the Sahasra- dala - padma (lotus) in himself. The activation of the pineal gland is believed to be the catalyst for heightened spiritual awareness. Joyful, heavenly hormones that pineal gland generate comes down via throat and spreads all over the body through the blood. Yogis describe this as Nectar/Elixir – 'Amruth,' which has taste of salty, bitterness and sweetness.

Yogis who experience this profound, otherworldly taste achieve a state of being where they are unaffected by the passage of time, aging, diseases, or infirmities. He is the embodiment of bliss and attains immortality. To achieve this ultimate, incomparable, and complete state of bliss within one's current lifetime is the very goal that every yogi strives for through dedicated yogic practices.

Divinity prevails in a Yogi who has attained a state of Samadhi, and this state reflects a profound manifestation of godliness within him. At this stage, Godliness flows through him. He IS God Himself. By mere intention he can make things happen, who is the Master of creation, preservation and destruction. He IS the Centre of the Universe and powers of Nature follows his intentions/instructions. Nothing is impossible for him. No law of this world is binding to him. His synchronization with the universal wavelength allows him to embody and wield the collective powers of Nature.

Well known legendary story of churning of Palazhi is nothing but a storyline depicting this. Pranayama (breath control) is metaphorically described as the "churning" of one's internal energy.The practitioner connects the three primary energy channels—Ida, Pingala, and Sushumna along the spine (Mount Meru) using controlled breath (symbolized by the serpent Vasuki). As a result of this vigorous internal practice, the practitioner may experience the manifestation of profound spiritual insights or symbolic forms, such as Kamadhenu. At the end, the nectar appears. The yogi who consumes this nectar attains immortality. He IS God now. He is Brahma Njani – knower of supreme knowledge of ultimate reality – the embodiment of 'Sat-cit-ānanda.

Manthra Sadhana

Systematic and dedicated spiritual practice of repeatedly chanting or meditating on a specific mantra, usually under the guidance of a Guide (Guru).

Those who embark on a spiritual path have typically engaged in some form of mantra sadhana (spiritual practice involving mantras). There are specific yoga traditions where practitioners incorporate mantra sadhana as a key element. Systems such as Vasi yoga, Hamsa yoga, and Kundalini yoga each utilize specific Beeja Mantras (seed syllables).

The stillness of the mind, characterized by the cessation of mental chatter, is attained through Pranayama practice, when one achieves the state of Kevala Kumbhaka. This involves the spontaneous retention of the breath, where the external and internal movement of breath is naturally suspended. The practice of Kevala Kumbhaka is considered as an advanced yogic technique, crucial for deep spiritual development. Manthra practitioners attempt to achieve this state by employing the mantras in a specific way.

In mantra sadhana, practitioners utilize a specific regulation of sound to still the mind. The repetitive utterance of the same sound or syllable, combined with focused concentration on the mantra, leads to the mind's regulation. This process gradually reduces the stream of thoughts, ultimately resulting in mental stillness. In a deep, tranquil state, breath naturally halts in Kevala Kumbhaka, a profound breath retention where the mind achieves singular focus, using mantra as a tool for this intense concentration, leading to deeper stillness and awareness. The focused repetition of a chosen deity's name or the contemplation of their various forms can both effectively calm the mind and cultivate a state of concentrated focus. Therefore, chanting divine names or mantras is a risk-free practice for common people, even if mistakes are made.

It is essential to be attentive when reciting a mantra or the name of a deity because the specific arrangement of sounds and words is considered a precise formula, designed to have a subtle, inherent effect on the practitioner, rather than merely being a technique for mental regulation. Mantras work by creating specific sound vibrations that travel through the nervous system and resonate in particular areas of the body. This is why it's considered essential to chant mantras with extreme precision and care. The sacred syllables are often described as being like a precisely aimed shot that travels with focus and intensity. To achieve the full benefits of the practice, the nama recitation must be performed while synchronizing with the specific breathing pattern; otherwise, it will only yield the general effects associated with simple chanting.

Sound travels more quickly and with greater intensity through water than it does through air, leading one to speculate about the impact of mantra sound waves within the human body, which is approximately 70% water.

Have already explained in detail about the Aadhara chakra and about petals and how the Beeja Manthras function In Kundalini Yoga, elsewhere.

The capacity of sound to influence the human mind is a shared element utilized by a diverse group of individuals: singers, dancers, and musicians actively harness this influence in their performances. Connoisseurs, in turn, leverage this very same ability to appreciate and enjoy these artistic expressions. When a singer modulates their sound in harmony with the vocal movement, their mind becomes completely absorbed in the subtle nuances and emotional depth of the music. Furthermore, because singing inherently requires breath control, it provides a similar experience and benefits to practicing the yogic discipline of pranayama, the practice of conscious breathing.

How should Manthra sadhana be practiced?

Whichever spiritual practice one follows, the Guru plays a central role, providing the practitioner with a specific mantra and method tailored to their path. The practitioner is expected to diligently follow these instructions, as the Guru emphasizes the importance of strict adherence to the prescribed practice. This guidance is considered crucial for the practitioner's spiritual progress. The general steps and crucial considerations for Mantra Sadhana viz. preparation, mindset and practice shall be explained now in detail.

In Mantra sadhana, the syllables or letters within a mantra are to be connected to one of three states: prana (inhalation), apana (exhalation) or kumbhaka (the suspended state of breath between the two). The recitation of the mantra requires precise synchronization of each letter or syllable with the breath cycle (inhalation, exhalation, or breath retention). This must be performed in a worshipful manner, strictly adhering to the specific breathing instructions provided by your spiritual teacher (Guru). "Mantropasana," a practice intrinsically linked to the breath, facilitates the integration of Pranayama with Mantra sadhana or mantra recitation. Performing mantra sadhana in this specific manner significantly enhances its effectiveness.

Stages of Manthra sadhana

Manthra sadhana should be set in motion by sitting restfully upright in a posture (asana), keeping head and body straight. First stage is to recite manthra loudly, by controlling the breath as advised by the Guru. Once it is recited- number of times as specified- the sound waves travels all over the body and systemizes the body by bringing in balance. During this practice, it is common for the practitioner to feel vibrations or a tingling sensation extending throughout their entire body.

In the second stage, the same manthra is recited internally, inaudible outside. As the mantra reaches the subtle levels of the body, its deeper influence takes hold. At this stage, it is imperative to strictly follow the breath pattern. Following this method and reciting specified times will result in whole-body vibration. At the next stage, the recitation of the mantra transcends both audible and inaudible verbalization, becoming a perpetual internal resonance, heard continuously within one's mind. We only need to be receptive, absorb and merge into the inner quietude. This is the third stage of Manthra sadhana. At this stage the practitioner gets mastery of Manthra, ie, Self Realization. The purpose of practice is now accomplished. He attains ineffable/inexpressible state of Joyfulness -the Samadhi state.

Different Stages of Awakening of Kundalini Chakra - Enlightenment – signs/qualities

Achieving spiritual emancipation through Yoga is a structured process, with the practitioner advancing progressively through each stage of the practice. When a yogi initiates and consistently maintains uninterrupted yoga practices, the positive effects will become apparent in a short time. A profound enhancement in your overall well-being and inner state will lead to the emergence of peace; mental focus will improve, and tranquility will become an apparent, natural condition. Concentration becomes stronger and more focused, and the reduction in excessive thoughts allows for a profound experience of peace and serenity. Inner turmoil subsides, replaced by a profound sense of tranquility and blissfulness. Attachment for material possessions and worldly pleasures will get reduced and mind turns inward to find out one's true essence or identity. Mind at that stage reaches its own sanctuary. Celestial glow/divine radiance will increase and the spiritual aura will be visible to everyone who interacts with him. Yogi can experience the purification and cleansing of his own breath.

The sound will be crystal clear. Communication will be impactful, succinct, and genuine. Uncomplicated words, yet powerful enough to explain spiritual experience in a simple way. No effort is needed to make the truth clear.The energy emanating from the Yogi radiates to those sitting nearby, allowing them to also experience immense joy.

These are all indicators of spiritual progress, the fruits that a spiritual practitioner (sādhaka) typically achieves through dedicated practice. One can personally verify and ascertain the phases by analyzing the increase of one's own spiritual energy, which has been dormant all these years. Also, the changes it brings in one's body and mind in each stage which act as indicators. Although individuals may report similar general spiritual experiences, the specific nature of these experiences is likely to vary at a subtle level because everyone has a unique nervous system and different habitual tendencies. When a person channels their energy upwards, they encounter various obstacles in that flow. The nature of these very obstacles dictates the specific spiritual experiences they will have. Also,the method used to achieve this varies depending on the individual.

This can be further clarified with an example. Spiritual advancement among followers of the path of devotion (Bhakti Yoga), the path of wisdom (Jnana Yoga), or the path of action (Karma Yoga) may not be as readily apparent or progress at the same pace as those following other branches of the path of yoga. In the path of yoga, it is posited that practitioners who engage in intense Kundalini Yoga sadhana—incorporating specific pranayama, mudras, and bandhas—may experience a more rapid progression toward their spiritual goal compared to those who follow the traditional eight limbs of Ashtanga Yoga. Moreover, even when individuals use the same practice methods, their progress pace may vary because each nervous system has a unique natural resistance, influenced by what is referred to as 'samskarik play'. Spiritual experiences are inherently subjective and personal, which naturally leads to a wide variety of interpretations and explanations.This diversity can create confusion among those seeking or practicing spirituality. The conviction that one's own system is best is born purely of personal experience; other people's different experiences are equally true for them as their personal learning. So, differences of opinion regarding spiritual experiences are not a cause for concern. Variations in our personal experiences, compared to those of others, do not indicate a faulty path; they simply reflect our individual differences.

It is already established that chakras function as key convergence points within the body's expansive nervous system, which branches out into various divisions and sections. The primary chakra system involves seven energy points, starting with the foundational Root (Muladhara) at the base, moving up through the Sacral (Svadhisthana), Solar Plexus (Manipura), Heart (Anahata), Throat (Vishuddha), and Third Eye (Ajna), culminating in the spiritual Crown (Sahasrara) chakra. Since Sahasrara, envisioned as the thousand-petaled lotus (Sahasra-dala-Padma), is often not classified merely as a chakra in the same way as the lower energy centers, but rather seen as the seat of supreme consciousness. When the Kundalini energy ascends the Sushumna Nadi, it activates and spiritually awakens the associated nerve cells. This energy movement produces swirling forces similar to magnetic fields, which can be felt by a practitioner. These energetic swirls are the reason each nerve center is conceptualized as a chakra. When the removal of obstacles allows the Kundalini energy to reach and awaken the nerve centers, the practitioner experiences the effects of that awakening. Typically, obstacles are often encountered at each of the six centers (chakras), and the Kundalini energy proceeds upward only after these blockages are cleared. However, this is not a universal experience; some practitioners may find that certain chakras are already open, allowing the energy to pass these points without obstruction. This unique experience might lead such an individual to a different concept regarding the precise count or necessity of all six chakras. When we clearly understand that personal experience is paramount, any apprehension or disputes about Yoga Shastra disappear.

This discussion will now focus on the process of Kundalini awakening, charting its ascent to the Sahasrāra and examining the transformative changes this journey brings to the practitioner. This information will provide a framework for understanding and contextualizing one's personal experiences.

When Kundalini awakens – First stage

Sadhakas (spiritual practitioners) involved in yogic practices with a practical understanding will experience the cumulative physical and mental effects of these practices with each passing day. Yogasanas foster a flexible and agile body, with muscles becoming both pliable and strong. Through consistent practice, individuals gain mastery over their physical form, finding that previously challenging asanas can be performed with ease and lightness. He will be able to sit for a longer period in many of the postures, especially in Padmasan, Vajrasan, and Sukhasan, without any effort.

When an individual begins a regular practice of various Pranayama techniques, their physical and mental conditions are likely to improve significantly.This practice may lead to an increase in spiritual brilliance and inner strength, while minor physical and mental afflictions may also disappear rapidly. As a practitioner advances in Pranayama, the nervous system will purify, and energy will flow more freely. With the lungs reaching their full potential, breathing will transform - becoming noticeably cleaner, deeper, and more refined. This full capacity allows prana to permeate every corner of the body, nourishing areas that were once out of reach. A marked reduction in the rate of breathing diminishes rush of thoughts, leading to a profound, unprecedented state of serenity. Yogi's inner tranquility significantly enhances his social interactions. This state of calm enables him to engage harmoniously with others and manage issues and crises with notable composure.The result is a mind characterized by exceptional clarity and serenity.

When Pranayama kriyas like Bhastrika kindles inner fire, yogi starts experiencing higher states of yogic consciousness.This practice increases both internal and body temperature. As a result, the yogi experiences deep, comfortable, and highly restful sleep. The need for prolonged rest is diminished, and the overall duration of sleep gets reduced because short periods of 'micro sleep' are sufficient for complete rejuvenation. This state is not sleep deprivation. The individual will awaken feeling energized and without any tiredness. He comes out of sleep refreshed and energetic.

Since the internal heat generated by the impact of Pranayama kriyas is concentrated in the abdominal region, it leads to thorough digestion and complete nutrient absorption. Consequently, a yogi's requirement for food intake will get reduced.

When the nervous system reaches a sufficient level of purity, the dormant Kundalini energy within a Yogi becomes active. The inner fire spreads in the abdomen area, one can feel a movement that is as thin as a hair and half the length of index finger, moves rapidly downwards; as a serpent that got beaten up moves to its burrow at a lightning speed. A significant, vital energy channel is awakened at the navel; this allows the previously dormant energy to cascade downward in waves, leading to a profound inner experience. This experience is attributed to the awakening of the Kundalini, a vital energy mentioned specifically in all Yoga methods. The relevance of the serpent symbolism is that the sādhaka experiences the movement of energy - often associated with the awakening of kundalini energy - as being as swift as that of a serpent. Coinciding with this internal sensation,the seeker feels a notable expansion or opening in the navel region. When the pranic energy reaches previously untouched areas, he experiences such a sensation.

At the coccygeal region (the bottom end of the sacrum/spine), one may feel a localized intensification of heat. The Sadhaka experiences the Mooladhara area warming up. This sensation is akin to focusing solar energy through a lens to heat a concentrated point. The starting point of the Sushumna Nadi is the small opening at the end of the sacrum bone, through which this vital nerve or energy channel emerges from the spinal column. The perineum itself is considered the center of the Mooladhara chakra. By concentrating one's focus (centering) on this point, internal heat is intensified. The Kundalini energy, which is originating from the navel region (swathishtana), then opens the corresponding base of the Sushumna Nadi and ascends the spinal column. Though a sādhaka may experience the general force (momentum) of Kundalini energy, they might not yet perceive its specific, direct ascent or spurt through the Sushumna nadi after initially activating the base chakra (Mooladhara). In some, the process of the Mooladhara breaking or activating, and the subsequent rush of Kundalini energy upwards, is experienced as an instantaneous and powerful surge, akin to a bolt of lightning. Due to the purified state of the subtle energy channels (nadis) and the powerful awakening of Kundalini energy, all blockages in the path are cleared, allowing the energy to rise through and open the shadadharas and reach the Sahasrara Chakra.

Second Stage

The ascent of Kundalini energy, once it pierces the Mooladhara chakra and enters the Sushumna nadi, is a gradual process. Its progression upward through each successive chakra typically spans days, months, or even years. The speed of this spiritual journey is contingent upon both the 'sadhaka's' (practitioner's) intensity of practice, type of practice and the purity of their subtle energy channels (nadis). Some souls may require more than one lifespan to fully realize their potential or purpose.

Localized heat in the Sushumna indicates a trapped state for the Kundalini energy. Releasing the perceived blockage facilitates its upward movement to the next chakra in the system.That is, the point where the heat is now concentrated, the Kundalini energy has reached and it has moved up from the chakra where the experience was that of crispy; fresh and cool, invigorating.

As the Kundalini energy ascends from the Mooladhara chakra to the Swadhisthana chakra, the perceived sensation transitions from a feeling of coolness at the Mooladhara to warmth at the Swadhisthana. When the Kundalini energy activates and moves beyond the Mooladhara, the sadhaka's consciousness becomes singularly focused on that specific energy center. As this energy ascends through Sushumna Nadi, awareness simultaneously rises in alignment with it.

When Pranayama practice is continued, Kundalini energy enters the Swadhishtana chakra, activating it and causing a swirl of energy to emerge. It's like a chakra we light during religious events; spinning, ground-based firework, often called a 'chakra', because its motion resembles that of a turning wheel. That is why shadadharas are called chakras.

Upward travel of Kundalini energy after breaking through each chakras above and reaching Vishudhi chakra, is the second stage. Starting from the navel area and breaking through Mooladhara is the first stage. It is important to recognize that when the Kundalini energy awakens and settles in a specific center, our consciousness and focus follow suit, centering there as well. The breaking (or activation/opening) of each chakra bestows spiritual accomplishments and mystical powers, known as siddhis, upon the sadhaka. However, to continue on the path of spiritual progress, the practitioner must not become attached to these powers and must move beyond them. The journey of Kundalini energy is straightforward as it ascends from the Muladhara up to the Vishuddhi chakra. However, guiding the energy beyond the Vishuddhi is thought to be significantly more challenging, demanding more advanced, intense, and esoteric practices. This is the third stage of Practice.

Third stage

Through esoteric and powerful practices, the upward movement of Kundalini energy from the Vishuddha chakra activates the Ajna chakra, thereby elevating the sadhaka to the highest states of spirituality. Ajna chakra, also known as Third Eye, gets activated. Awareness centers in the Third eye. Physical eyes get locked in the centre of eye brows. This is called Shambhavi Mudra (gaze inward on the point between the eye brows). Initially, focusing attention at the point between eyebrows was difficult. Now, it is challenging to move attention away from there;

eyes and awareness are almost magnetically drawn to that 'third eye' area. The sadhak enters a profound state of meditation. It is easy to sit mindfully with closed eyes and maintain awareness for extended periods. With continued meditative practice, an inherent channel develops, guiding the Kundalini force toward the Sahasrara center. As a result, Sahasra-Dala-Padma gets opened (blooms). The

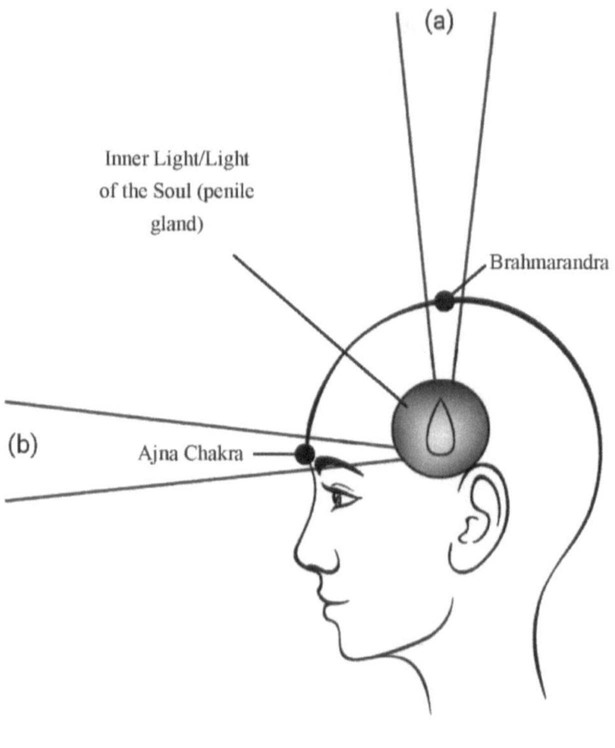

(a) Upward flow of energy through Brahmarandra
(b) Forward flow of energy through Ajna Chakra

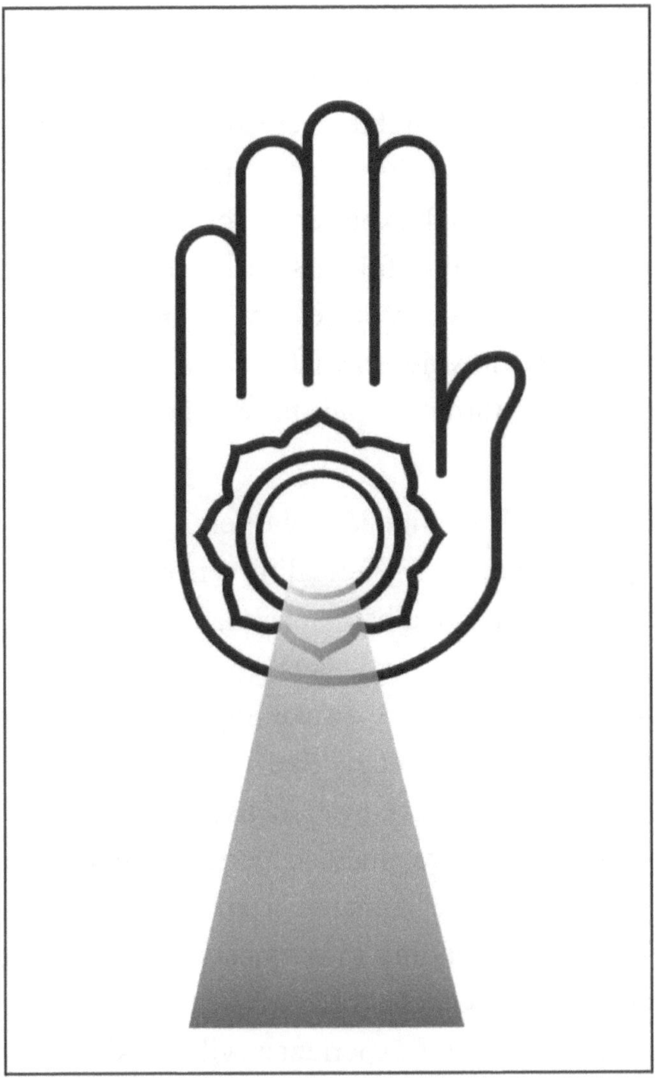

spiritual seeker's awareness settles in the center of their

head, becoming as still and bright as a lamp's flame.The yogi then perceives the 'Light of the Soul' or 'Self' and achieves the deep meditative state of Samadhi.

A profound coolness settles across the forehead, while a radiant sense of enlightenment illuminates the mind. This internal stillness ushers in a supreme state of bliss, a universally desired experience for the yogi. The state of Satchitananda - blissful existence - for which there is no substitute and is irreplaceable, is now his reality. The nectar starts flowing down from the Sahasra-dala -Padma through the throat. Yogi tastes the nectar and attains immortality.

It was mentioned earlier that the upward rising/ascension of Kundalini energy starts with the opening of Mooladhara chakra. Significant phase of spiritual rise of Yogi gets initiated at this instance. Outcomes of spiritual awakening start exhibiting in the body and mind of Yogi; like never before. A yogi who achieves the breaking (activation/opening) of the Mooladhara chakra may experience his awareness as moving out of the Annamaya kosha (physical body/food sheath) and expanding to permeate the other, more subtle layers of the panchakosha system that lie within the physical layer. The experience will be similar to a snake shedding its skin, a process known as ecdysis, involving the casting off of the outermost layer of its body. No perceptible change will be visible in the physical body, however, in the subtle level, yogi feels that the outermost layer has been removed and his body has now reached another level which is more subtle, fresh and pure. Yogi feels a profound sense of renewal, as though he has undergone a complete personal transformation. Each morning, he awakens with the same sensation of freshness and purity one might experience after emerging from a cleansing bath.

Spiritual experiences inherently defy linguistic description; words are insufficient to detail their significance, purpose, or the feelings involved.The subtle dimensions that are part of these experiences are beyond explanations. Can anyone compare and explain about the sweetness of sugar and honey? Self-knowledge can only be acquired through direct experience. This record of spiritual journeys is merely intended to offer guidance to others on their personal quest.

Yogi achieves a critical stage of spiritual experience when the divine energy, having ascended and broken through the Ajna chakra, enters the Sahasrara chakra located at the crown of the head. He understands, awareness has narrowed to a singular point in the center of the head, a focal point no larger than a grain (pineal gland). He perceives his true self as a radiant, steadfast flame. In this experience, the distinction between the one who observes and what is being observed has vanished; they have merged into a single reality. This state represents the merging of the individual consciousness (Atman) with the universal consciousness (Brahman). He speaks directly with the Absolute and has merged into that state of being, becoming a living embodiment of Ultimate Reality through self-knowledge. Now, He is the centre of this world. He is the Master of creation, sustenance and dissolution. He is the source of all creation, which comes into existence solely through His will and intention. The existence and maintenance of everything depend entirely on His wish. Ultimately, all things dissolve back into Him. He is the sovereign Lord, the ruler of all realms and worlds. The veil that had been covering the perceptions is now removed and understanding has dawned. He holds absolute sway over all occurrences in this world. He has the same attributes as God; the Omnipotent and Omniscient.

Countless nerve cells that are centered on the left and right side of Kapala region are now purified and flowing with prana. This synchronized energetic activation awakens countless nerve cells and energy points to facilitate the realization of their highest potential, leading to a state of heightened awareness and spiritual awakening. Brahmaranthra is now in open state. The divine energy now flows upwards through the central energy channel along the spine moving past the Brahmaranthra in a form of circular column, head of which is kept downwards, that has embarked from the crown of head. Similarly, another stream of divine energy embarking from the same point, flows in the form of circular column, horizontally positioned, through the Third eye. These two streams- Vertical and horizontal- converge in Sahasra-Dala-Padma. In other words, it starts from the same point. Yogi now maintains a continuous state of open-indedness and receptivity, perceiving the world with a boundless, unburdened mind. His consciousness has become attuned to frequencies beyond this world. With the palm chakras activated, pranic energy is powerfully and consistently released. When he extends his hand, one can feel waves of energy wash over the body; it is this same powerful emanation that radiated from the palms of Saints such as Sree Sathya Sai Baba.

A yogi who has attained awakening experiences an internal effulgence on which his meditation effortlessly continues; no conscious effort is needed for concentration as his focus occurs automatically.

As the mind transcends the physical state through continued meditation, the Yogi experiences a profound union with the inner light, ascending to elevated stages of Samadhi. Since my understanding does not encompass the higher states of spiritual awakening, which are the domain of accomplished Masters; consequently, I must respectfully decline to elaborate on them. The only path available to us is through the study of books written by enlightened individuals.

Conscious Liberation from the body (Dehamukthi)

The path to liberation culminates in Samadhi, a state of deep meditative consciousness that brings ultimate freedom and bliss. Liberation from the body (Dehamukthi) is achieved by a Yogi who has ascended the path of Yoga, after entering the state of Samadhi, and who takes out his own Prana (life force) through the Brahmarandra voluntarily.The concept of Svecchāmrtyu, the ability to consciously choose the time and manner of one's death, is described as an ability attained solely by those who have reached the advanced spiritual state of Samadhi. This is the act of a yogi consciously and intentionally leaving their physical body at a chosen time and place, having complete awareness of the process. Normally, life goes out in unconscious state. Mostly, life goes out through the eyes. Abrupt ending of life because of accidents/unnatural/violent deaths etc., the soul leaves the body through openings in the lower part of the body. Under these conditions, the soul's rebirth would be on a lower plane of existence. Despite life going out through the eyes, he cannot escape the wheel of Existence; the cycle of birth and death.

Reincarnated as a human from the ancestral sphere, a person's life is shaped by his karma, and he must live through the consequences of his actions (karma phala). Whether it offers an opportunity for spiritual realization or is a lower incarnation is determined by the karma accumulated from actions in a previous life.

However, a Yogi who embraces Svecchāmrtyu (the conscious choice of death) allows their soul to exit the body through the Brahmarandhra (the crown aperture) and ascend to Devaloka, the celestial home of divine beings. The physical body is left behind in the material world. However, in the highest state of yoga, a Master of the ten life forces (pancha vayu and upa-pranas) can consciously leave his physical form by retaining Dhananjaya, the upa-prana that lingers in the body after death that is associated with decomposition. Therefore, the body of a yogi who has attained liberation will not decompose even after years of preservation. Devotees keep the body in a tomb with special preparations. The divine energy radiates around these Samadhi tombs/shrines. A person with subtle vision can experience this divine radiance.The memorials built over these Samadhis subsequently became prominent shrines/temples. Many places of worship like Ettumanoor, Vaikom, Sree Padmanabha Swami Temple, Trivandram, Palani are Mahasamadhis of great Sidhas. Idols of personal Gods (Ishta devatha) of these Sidhas are also seen in some shrines. Within the temple premises itself these memorials are preserved and protectedIn some locations, these memorials were transformed into major shrines.

Not all individuals who seek self-realization outside of the discipline of Yoga achieve the state of Yoga Samadhi. Likewise, not everyone who follows the Yoga path necessarily reaches Samadhi. When they leave their body, on the assumption that they have reached Samadhi state, we arrange Samadhi tombs to keep the body. We must know, these places do not radiate divine energy. They are mere tombs only. Because of ignorance we consider them as Maha samadhis.

Formless Samadhi (Aroopa Samadhi) liberation as light body

A Yogi who has achieved the highest state of consciousness and mastery over their own being can, at will, initiate the process of death, wherein the physical body systematically dissolves into its five elemental components (Pancha Boothas). The individual's Soul (Atma), now a brilliant light or effulgence, is intentionally released to unite with the Supreme Reality (Brahmam). This profound and conscious exit from the physical realm is known as liberation after death or Vidheha Mukti. The traditional belief regarding the Great Siddhas is that they eventually achieve the state of Parabrahmam (the Supreme Reality) as Atma Jyothi, a divine light possessing the brilliance of a thousand suns. Over time, it is held that their physical bodies diminish and either completely vanish or are transformed into sacred ash. Records show that even in the recent past, cases in which Yogis entered a state of Samadhi inside sealed rooms, only for their bodies to have vanished when the chambers were officially reopened.This event is attributed to vidheha mukti, or physical liberation after death. Buddhist monks in Tibet and elsewhere practice techniques aimed at achieving liberation, known as deha mukti or videha mukti. These methods, sometimes performed as special rituals, are used in the presence of others to attain spiritual liberation. These blessed souls can take any form/incarnate and can appear in front of us or, without incarnation can work on us at subtle level. They are the Avadhoothas who incarnate to bless us all and work for the well-being of the humanity. We should be virtuous enough to receive their blessings.

How can an enlightened person be identified?

When picturing an enlightened or awakened person, the image of Sree Buddha often comes to mind: eyes half-closed in contemplation, a face radiating profound serenity and compassion. This archetypal form, appearance, and demeanor have become synonymous with the attainment of enlightenment. Across how many generations/cultures has the image of the Buddha - a being of infinite compassion and wisdom - been represented in art and idols? The distinctive features of an enlightened being (Bodhisattva) are often reflected in the masterful craftsmanship of Buddha idols.

Numerous enlightened individuals continue to live among us. Even those without knowledge of advanced spiritual states like yoga or Samadhi can often perceive a unique quality in a person who has attained spiritual awakening. This distinction is thought to be so clear that it is perceptible even to animals. Stories are sometimes told of wild animals coexisting peacefully with Avadhoota Siddhas, enlightened beings who have reached the highest spiritual states, the animals behaving as if they were domesticated. This phenomenon highlights a perceived harmony and connection with nature achieved by these highly realized souls. In the Buddhacharita, Devadatta, Buddha's jealous cousin, unleashed the intoxicated, ferocious elephant Nalagiri to trample Buddha, but the Buddha's boundless loving-kindness subdued the beast, causing it to halt its charge and kneel submissively before Him; a powerful display of compassion's triumph over violence. Many people have observed instances where venomous snakes coexist peacefully with yogis around their ashram grounds, and occasionally even on their bodies. It is known to us that dogs always stayed with the well-known Avadhotha, Mayiyamma. Amma ate and slept with them. Boundless, unconditional compassion and profound love flowing out of the enlightened souls attract all living beings towards them. Human frailties, flaws, or imperfections that are considered a natural or inescapable part of the human condition cease to exist and all these enlightened souls become embodiment of love and compassion. The divine presence or inherent quality of enlightened Masters naturally draws all living beings to them, as everyone desires their nearness and intimacy. A sense of tranquility and calmness that cannot be found anywhere else is felt in their presence. By the splendor of their lofty energy field, everything around them gets purified. The state or place described, where one experiences profound peace, a cessation of worries, intense longing to be present, and a desire never to leave, is where one feels God's presence.

Worldly pursuits and material gains such as job, wealth, family, and power hold little significance for a spiritually awakened person who has experienced divine presence. Because of their presence, many individuals become devoted followers of the sidhas. Large numbers of people gather around these revered figures, motivated by a strong desire to personally experience their boundless love, make physical contact, and hear their calming wisdom. It becomes difficult to leave such an esteemed presence. The attractiveness of a yogi who is immersed in unearthly, supernatural blissful state understands and distinguishes inner consciousness of all beings. These extremely subtle and spiritual vibrations touch our souls.The taste of ambrosial state - Sat-Chit-Ananda - brings us closer to him. The blissful state itself is the microscope to identify a Brahmanjan.

A Yogi's gaze radiates with an abundance of compassion, the purity of childlike innocence, and a deep, inherent bliss. Brilliance and purity in the eyes are the manifestations of Yogi's spiritual attainment. While a common man's eyes mirror the world's turmoil. A Yogi's eyes reflects void-like inner state and immeasurable bliss. Boundless love and compassion wells up the eyes. We can experience the eyes that hold the brilliant, open vastness of a cloudless sky, as infinite as the universe. They are filled with godliness. A deep serenity, mirroring the tranquil sea settles there. They are no more of this world. The charm and elegance of the other world entices those eyes. Divine grace envelops them. Their gentle, emanating aura reaches the depths of our souls, cleansing them. All is cleansed in the path of the light. Those indefensible eyes reach places that are subtle and gross. All secrets get revealed in front of them. He possesses infinite knowledge. He is omniscient.

In Yogavidhya, those who have attained Yoga hood are often described as 'Oodwarethan', meaning one who has sublimated sexual energy; a celibate- one who can make the semen flow upwards. It is assumed, the semen flows upward through the Sushmna, from its source and reaches brain/crown chakra. The essence of this assumption is that Yogi experiences indescribable, transcendental blissfulness when the semen reaches the brain. Physiological verification would render this assumption unscientific. We cannot interpret ancient principles literally. In all these hymns, poetic language is generally used. Hence, when a seeker engages in superficial reading, he may get entrapped in the literal meaning. Pranic energy that is in the human body is being lost through the nine gates in the body - navadwara. Gravitation draws energy flow downwards too. Yogi, through methods that are esoteric and profound, blocks the flow of energy through the nine gates of body and changes the course to the reverse direction. In whose body the energy flow leaves its natural direction and rises upwards, is called 'Oodwarethan'. Here it is implied that bio-energy, not semen, moves upwards. In the presence of enlightened masters, their command over energy naturally influences the flow in their surroundings, allowing attendees to share in their powerful, transformative experiences. For the average person, blinking is a frequent, involuntary action that occurs without conscious effort or attention, and attempting to control it is challenging. However, enlightened Yogis possess the ability to control this natural reflex; they can sit for extended periods, even hours, without blinking, effortlessly sustaining this state in a manner that is distinct from most people. He masters prana that controls body activities and thereby acquires this super- normal power to achieve mastery over his own prana through intense practice effectively that subdues all the lesser vayus in the body.

The soul speaks most eloquently through the eyes is a well known statement. The thoughts and emotions that go through internally reflect in the eyes. In the state of a Yogi who has achieved samadhi through the complete stilling of the mind and emotions, the boundless reflection of infinite expanse and supreme bliss becomes apparent. Inner tranquility manifests outwardly as an unwavering, still gaze in enlightened individuals. The rapid blinking of eyes is often interpreted as a sign of an unsettled or restless mind. The very use of a term like 'whimsical women' points to such a state. In contrast, a tranquil and focused mind is reflected in eyes that are steady, clear, and serene. A troubled mind often manifests as restless or tense body movements. Similarly, inner turmoil can be reflected in one's physical demeanor and gestures. As the mind fluctuations increases body also become restless. Achieving a state of mental stillness and physical ease appears deceptively simple until you actually try to do it. True physical stillness is a reflection of a tranquil mind; subtle movements persist until mental serenity is achieved. The body will continue to exhibit subtle movements no matter how hard one tries to keep it still, unless the mind first attains a state of complete calm.

A yogi seeking mental tranquility should initially focus on maintaining physical stillness. This is precisely why asanas (physical postures) are a fundamental and important part of yoga practice. Before starting meditation (dhyana), a foundational step is to achieve steadiness and comfort in a physical posture (asana). This process requires practicing different poses to discover and ultimately settle into a stable, sustainable position that aligns with your individual body's needs. Yogi who sustains a perfect posture achieves a state where the body is entirely at rest, even while the body remains fully awake and alert. The interconnectedness of the body and mind means that even minimal physical movement can disrupt mental stillness, making it difficult to establish a state of meditative absorption (dhyana). Physical movement affects mind and the mental activity affects the body also.

The body of a Knower of Brahman (a Brahma jnani) who has achieved complete equanimity is often described as being in a state of perfect stillness, utterly devoid of ordinary physical agitation or reactive movement. It will also be in total resting state. When an individual achieves a state of profound stillness and enlightenment, the conventional interdependence of body and mind is transcended. The inherent mind-body connection gets severed. Thereafter, even when the body movement happens, it will have no impact on the mind of Yogi. In all circumstances, whether active or at rest, he maintains a state of total mental stillness and profound calm. Therefore he is called Sthithapranjan – a person of steady wisdom, free from worldly attachments and aversions. There will be a visible rhythm and fluidity in his body movements. When he walks it's like he is gliding. His body and mind are completely tranquil. A profound sense of tranquility pervades his being. When contrasted with the fluidity of his body movement, our own can feel mechanical and unnatural, almost robotic. The enduring fluidity in the body movements of the famous Malayalam actor, Mohanlal, remains a notable observation. His tranquil demeanor might suggest to observers a man in a spiritual plane. The description is intended solely to convince observers of the Yogi's tranquility.

Spiritual progress is observed when the Kundalini energy ascends, moving beyond the Vishuddhi chakra.The practitioner's voice becomes more refined and clear as they elevate the energy associated with this chakra. It becomes stereophonic; if we use a modern term. Once he masters the manipulation of sound frequencies, he can effortlessly traverse the complete musical spectrum, from the highest treble to the lowest bass. Spiritual vitality and authenticity oozes out in each word that he pronounces. It becomes so pleasing to the ears. He speaks the language with effortless fluency. Acquiring strong communication skills is considered a natural talent and a divine gift. We stand awestruck and filled with wonder in the presence of those who are so gifted.Though lacking formal schooling, his utterances possess an innate wisdom and grace that many describe as divine, marking him as a person of true erudition. His pronouncements alone constitute the irrefutable truth and the singular, ultimate testimony. They are the inviolable Gospel, offering universal joy and awaited by all existence. His divine utterances elevate humanity to a state of divinity.

As a yogi commences yoga practices, subtle effects become apparent. The body may feel a sense of lightness, the overall weight may seem to lessen, and movement can become more effortless. A palpable energy(Aura) surrounds him, its growing intensity poised for universal recognition. The individual's appearance is marked by a noticeable radiance and enhanced complexion, suggesting a vibrant and healthy glow. He experiences a reduction in waste products, specifically a decrease in the quantity of body feces, along with a positive change in the amount and quality of sweat produced. A distinct and pleasant, "divine" scent is emitted from the body, replacing the typical human odors.

The Secrets of Pranayama described in Pathanjali Yogasuthra

The principle of Yoga asserts that through integrated physical and mental practices, one can achieve mental tranquility and elevate awareness (consciousness) to its highest level. The significance of Yoga is attaining the peak of consciousness. The terms Samadhi, Enlightenment, Self Realization, knowledge of Brahman describe the same profound state. In this state one can experience intense as well as absolute Blissfulness. This experience is akin to sexual climax, but is an everlasting and blissful experience of profound ecstasy; this state is what yogis universally strive to attain. There is nothing that can replace this blissful state. All earthly achievements provide only fleeting happiness, a joy that is temporary and incomparable to the profound experience of eternal bliss. The pleasure associated with acquiring an object often fades the moment it is obtained. Later, your attention shifts to the pursuit of something better. This becomes a serial story. In this material realm, seeking joy through physical things only deepens our entanglement in an inescapable circle of desire. This results in grief. Finding joy within ourselves is the best remedy for this. That is perpetual and the inherent state of all being. This is Sat-Chit-Ananda 'the nature of Reality. All yogic paths and methods lead us to this goal. While the end goal remains constant, the process and the supporting factors vary.

Though there are innumerable methods in Yoga Path viz. Raja Yoga, Kriya Yoga, Hatha Yoga, Thanthra Yoga, Swara Yoga (Shara Yoga), Shiva Yoga, Kundalini Yoga etc., only difference is in the methods (Kriyas) or the style adopted. The ultimate aim and the experiences the Yogi going through are intrinsically the same in the pursuit of spiritual realization.

The popular conception of Yoga widely known today is largely shaped by Ashtanga Yoga, a system that introduces practitioners to the philosophical framework outlined in Sage Patanjali's Yoga Sutras. Therefore, the purpose of this effort is to select several key suktas from the practice of Ashtanga Yoga and elucidate the profound secrets and deeper meanings encapsulated within them. It will help a Yoga practitioner to understand the philosophy behind the practice with a deeper insight into their path, while also confirming its scientific grounding. Therefore, this study focuses on key verses from the Sadhana Pada of Patanjali's Yoga Sutras, concentrating on essential principles to guide the practical path to self-realization, rather than analyzing every single aphorism.To gain a comprehensive understanding of the principles (sidhantas) contained within the sutras, the study of other relevant yoga literature will also be taken up.

Yoga : Chitta Vritti Nirodha: - 1 part, Suthra 2

Sage Pathanjali in the beginning itself states that yoga is the cessation (or quieting/controlling) of the fluctuations of the mind. Mind (manas), Intellect (buddhi), and Ego (Ahamkara) are considered the three components that, together, constitute Chitta. Chitta can be understood as the psychological Existence which encompasses Id, Ego, and Super-ego, or the divisions of the conscious mind, subconscious mind, and unconscious mind. The mind reflects the world perceived through the five knowledge senses and engages with that world through the five karma senses. The mind uses intelligence to analyze and distinguish information, operates through the senses; the instruments. It must be specifically noted that the Mind, Intelligence, and the Ego are not separate, independent entities or discrete, self-contained units. They are all part of different planes/dimensions of the spiritual essence. Consciousness passively takes in or perceives immediate sensory data, while intelligence actively interprets that data by comparing it to past knowledge, enabling understanding through discrimination and context. Unconscious mind works as the setting for these two. While the mind and intelligence are central to actions such as perceiving (knowing), analyzing, and operating, ego functions as the specific technique for understanding this entire knowing process. For example, when we see a table, in reality there is a table. Intelligence discerns that it is a table. There is a witness/ awareness that know that 'there is a table.' It is the wholeness of this process that is called mental activity/state of mind.

As the mind and intellect quiet down and thoughts subside, pure awareness—the witness—is all that remains. Controlling and stopping one's thoughts is precisely what is meant by chitta-vritti-nirodha, or the cessation of the mind's fluctuations. This doesn't stop thoughts from occurring; rather, it allows us to direct the thoughts that were previously beyond our control. We can choose to fully develop a nascent thought or to halt it the moment it appears. That means, the level of alertness has reached its maximum. Thoughts are like a bubble that expands as it ascends from the bottom of a vessel, ultimately bursting upon reaching the surface. How would it be if the rising of a bubble could be controlled anywhere, while it is ascending? Chitta-vritti-nirodha can similarly be defined as the complete control or regulation of the mind. The mind then acts as an organ, much like others, completely under the individual's command. We move the legs when we want to. But, we were to lose the volitional control to move the legs, it would fundamentally alter the experience of life and independence. When we want to sit at a place quietly, if the leg keeps moving, what it will be like? Normally, our mind reacts and acts automatically, without us having any control over its functioning. Chitta-vritti-nirodha is defined as the practice of bringing the uncontrolled mind under control. It is simply about keeping a tight rein on things. A horse without control runs wild, but with guidance, it can be managed. similar to this, mastery of your mind allows you to harness its complete power, effectively turning your mental capabilities into extraordinary skills.

How to bring about cessation or restraint of the changing states of mind - Chitta Vritti Nirodha

By achieving mastery over latent tendencies (vasanas) and consciously directing the life force (prana), one can quiet the incessant activity of the mind. – Soothram 71, Hatha yoga Pradipika

Latent tendencies (samskaras/vasanas) and the pulsation of vital force are the dual foundations upon which the Chitta exists. Regulation of one inherently facilitates the regulation of the other; consequently, Yogis specifically practice techniques aimed at regulating Prana. -Yoga Kundalini Upanishath

Yoga darshana expounded by Sage Pathanjali clearly states at the outset itself that Yoga is nothing but chita-vritti-nirodha. It is the state of being in which the ideational choice-making movement of mind slows down and comes to a stop. However, after stating that with practice and detachment this state can be achieved, the subsequent section proceeds directly to outlining the practical applications. The concept of Chita –vritti- nirodha (stilling the mind) is mentioned in detail within both the Hatha Yoga Pradipika and the Yoga Kundalini Upanishad as a necessary foundational practice for achieving higher states of yoga.

To understand these concepts more deeply, it is helpful to explore the nature of latent tendencies (samskaras) and life force (prana). Tendencies are, by definition, associated with innate urges to act in particular ways. It can be scientifically defined as the complete set of genes and genetic information (the genome) recorded at the most fundamental level within an organism, which orchestrates all its activities. As we have already established the specifics of these tendencies in depth, further discussion is not required. Our existence is intrinsically shaped by inherent tendencies that are beyond our direct conscious control.

The vibrations of vital forces or the flow of prana are equivalent to the flow of bio-magnetic energy within the body. Nerve impulses, which involve the flow of electric current, can be regulated. Pranayama is the practice of breath control, involving specific techniques for inhalation and exhalation to regulate the flow of life force or prana. Through the regulation of breath in Pranayama, one can work towards chitta-vritti-nirodha, which is the ultimate goal of stilling the mind's activity.

What is pranayama

'Pracchardana vidharanabhyam va pranasya'

Mental steadiness is attained by the expulsion and retention of breath (prana).

(Yogasuthram Samadahi padam soothram 34)

'Swasa praswasayorgathi vichathi pranayama'

Pranayama is the cessation/control of the movement of inhalation and exhalation.

(Yogasuthram Sadhana padam soothram 49)

Breathing is a continuous, lifelong process that sustains life from birth until death. This process involves three actions or stages. We inhale and exhale; in the pause between breaths, the activity momentarily ceases. Just as at the end of the inhale, a brief cessation in airflow occurs after exhaling and before the subsequent inhalation. In the context of yoga and spiritual practices (pranayama), the Sanskrit term pooraka refers to the conscious act of inhalation, while rechaka refers to the conscious act of exhalation. The brief break in between is known as kumbhaka which is breath retention or suspension of breath. So, there are two breaks in between inhalation and exhalation. The state of the lungs being full after inhalation is referred to as anthara kumbhakam and the state of lung empty after exhalation is called bahya kumbhakam. These are also known as pooraka kumbhakam and rechaka kumbhakam respectively. As long as breathing persists, so too will thoughts. That is why pulsations of vital force are the reason for ideational choice making movement of chitta. In the pause between breaths, the mind's activity slows down and comes to a complete halt. Cessation of breathing generally indicates irreversible stage of the dying process. What else is the way out? Spontaneous breath suspension between inhales and exhales is a natural feature of breathing. Just make these pauses longer. To increase Kumbhaka capacity, practice both internal and external breath retention by holding the nostrils closed for as long as comfortably possible after a deep inhalation and a complete exhalation. Wholehearted attention during the pauses causes the surge of thoughts to gradually subside. While breathing, hold your hand just below your nostrils to feel the flow of prana touching your palm. As you move your hand further away, you will notice the sensation on your palm begin to fade. It is possible to measure how far we are radiating our vital force. This will be different from person to person. Furthermore, duration of breathing can vary in a person from time to time. Breathing rate and depth increase with exertion (e.g., exercise, stress) and also sickness make breathing "longer" (more air, faster rate). As Kumbhaka practice deepens, inhalation and exhalation become so subtle they are only felt at the tip of the nostrils. With continued practice, your breathing will become centered at the spot inside the nostrils just below the eyebrows. The absolute cessation of both inhalation and exhalation is known as Kevala Kumbhaka. In this state, the mind becomes perfectly tranquil. This state, by pausing or breaking the flow of inhalation and exhalation is called Swasa praswasayorgathi vicchedah pranayamah (Pranayama is the regulation (cessation or pause) of the movement of inhalation and exhalation). Since Kevala Kumbhaka is inherently the state of Samadhi, the latter is impossible to attain without first mastering the former. At this stage, the mind and prana are irresistibly drawn to the Ajna Chakra, merging there as if pulled by a magnetic force. Upon reaching the pinnacle of tranquility and absolute awareness, the Yogi transcends into a state of pure witnessing. At last, the witness and the observed become one, entering a profound, hidden world to attain the elevated state of a Sidha.

All yoga paths in unison opine that without realizing Kumbhaka state- without breaking the habitual cycle of breathing in and out- no spiritual elevation happens. However, each path employs different practices to achieve this state. Each one practices what validates their doctrines. Comparing the validity of different paths is pointless. Yogis who attained Kevala Kumbhaka shared personal methods based on their direct experiences. Why reject or despise practices that have already demonstrated their efficacy through experience? This merely highlights the limited perspective and pride of those lacking deep spiritual insight. What one can do is to choose a path that fits him. This requires adherence to the practices prescribed by Masters/lineage holders.

In Pathanjali Yogasuthra

the Suthra 34 and 50, 51 in Samadhi pada describe what Pranayama is:

Suthra 34- in Samadhi pada- Pracchardana Vidharanabhyam Va-Pranasya (Prana can be controlled/ regulated by Exhalation and by breath retention/ suspension)

Suthra 50 - Bahybhyantara stambhavrttir desakala sankhyabhiparidrsto

Suthra 51 -Bahyabhyantaravisayaksepi chaturthah (The fourth pranayama is that which transcends the internal and external object.)

Grasping the concept of Prana is essential to unlocking the meaning of these sutras. Prana is often superficially equated with the breath, but its accurate, subtle definition refers to the universal, intelligent life force or vital energy that sustains all existence. In yoga, prana (life force) is the essential energy driving all physical and mental functions. This vital energy courses through the nervous system, empowering the function of every part of the body. There are ten of these which are rated as most important.

They are known as ten essential pranas or Dasha pranas.

(5 Pranas- (Prana, Apana, Samana, Udana, Vyana - governing major functions, and 5 Upa Pranas- Naga,

Kurma, Krikara, Devadatta, Dhananjaya). These are the nadis/meridians that conduct the flow of bio-energy throughout the body. Out of these, Prana and Apana serve as the two primary, foundational forces of life energy. Prana refers to the upward-moving energy in the body, while Apana is the downward-flowing energy. During inhalation, life force (prana) is drawn in through the nostrils, travels down, and settles. Mindful observation of the breath reveals this. At a basic level, we can call this Apana. During exhalation, the prana moves upward in the reverse direction, tracing a path behind the nostrils before exiting the body. This is Prana, the fundamental cosmic energy. It is reasonable to doubt whether this air is indeed Prana. It is the vital, cosmic energy inherent in the air that sustains all life. Since this force is directly felt in our daily lives, it is considered a synonym for Prana.

In light of this interpretation, let us examine the text of the suktham: Pracchardana Vidharanabhyam Va-Pranasya. Through the consistent, repeated practice of exhalation and retention in specific manner, we can deepen our understanding and integrate experiences. Prana is the vital energy or life force that is released. This, you internalize in a unique way. We will skip over that particular method for now. An enlightened Master's guidance is crucial for learning this. There is a School of thought that the ultimate teacher is the indwelling consciousness or the "Inner Self" located in you. Consequently, one can discover a personal method for internalization. Given the subtle and potent effects of Pranayama, it is considered unsafe to venture into the practice without proper guidance. Consider this a formal warning, as it is likely to cause physical or mental harm. However, the ultimate truth about Pranayama is that it must be internalized/adopted in a unique manner.

Now let us study the sukthas 50 and 51 - Bahybhyantara stambhavrttir desakala sankhyabhi paridrsto dirghasuksmah and Bahyabhyantara vishayakshepi chathurtah.

Though these two are shown as two different sukthas, it must be noted that the second one is continuation of the first one. The secret of Pranayama lies in making the stoppage of breath—both internal and external—prolonged and subtle, on the basis of place (desha), time (kala), and count (samkhya). Sutra 51 means that you can make your breath prolonged and subtle, without regard to place, time, or count (matra) and without any conditions. Practitioners of the initial interpretation practice Bahya and Antara Kumbhaka to make the breath more prolonged and subtle. This is what is called Bahya-sthambha- vruthi. To make their breathing longer and more subtle, practitioners of the second interpretation employ specific practices. This is called Abhyanthara-sthambha-vruthi. A shared outcome of these two practices is Kevala kumbhakam, which means stopping the breath (neither inhaling nor exhaling) while remaining comfortable and free of shortness of breath. To reach the Kevala kumbhaka state, practitioners in the first interpretation diligently and intensely practice prolonged external (Bahya kumbhakam) and internal (Anthara kumbhakam) breath retention. Instead of using force, proponents of second approach focus on achieving a state of Kevalakumbhaka automatically, leading to naturally extended breath retention. According to those who practice this method, Abhyanthra-sthambha -vruthi is taking prana internally up to Brahmarandhra and bring it to Kevala kumbhaka. Bahya-sthambha-vruthi is suspended breath control where the air is retained outside, leading toward the state of Kevala kumbhaka. According to one interpretation, Kevala Kumbhaka is known as Anthara-sthambha-vruthi because it is achieved by sealing the internal sensory nerves. Conversely, practitioners who focus on retaining breath outside the body, keeping prana external to the nerves, refer to this as Bahya-Kumbhaka-vruthi. While yogic paths like Vasi yoga, Kriya yoga, Hamsa yoga etc. practice this method, practitioners of Hatha yoga and thantric practices etc. concentrate more on practicing Kumbhakas the way mentioned in the first instance.

Now let us examine what is the time, place (in which part of the body prana is centered) and count.

Place

These are the spiritual energy centers or locations within the body where energy flows and where the mind can achieve deep, stable focus during meditation. Kalam (time) refers to the duration of a single breath cycle, including both inhalation, exhalation, and the pause between them. Samkhya denotes the breath counts or counts to complete a breath.

Pranayama based on energy centers involves visualizing the movement of prana from one specific chakra to another.

The time it takes to complete one breath is the basis for Kalam (speed).

For eg. Naadisudhy Pranayama - Sanghya, Bastrika & Kapalbathi – Kalam, Sidhavidya Pranayama – Desom, Vipasana – Vishayaakshepi (4th).

Samkhya refers to the number of times this is practiced or the breathing rate per minute or counts to complete a breath. Those who practice inhalation and exhalation to naturally extend and make their breath more subtle should focus on moving the prana from one specific chakra to another. For each sectarians, this visualization is different. As you practice this, your breath naturally slows, lengthening the duration of both inhalation and exhalation. Breathing becomes shallower or slower, at a particular time.

Hatha Yoga practitioners extend the duration of inhalation (Pooraka), exhalation (Rechaka), and retention (Kumbhaka) in order to adhere to the principles of place (Desha), time (Kala), and number (Sankhya).

By fixing attention only on the breath, this Pranayama can be practiced without concern for Desha (location), Kala (time), or Sankhya (count). This practice is known as Bhahyabhyanthara Vishayakshepeechaathurtha. (It is not merely holding the breath (Kumbhaka) but a state where the practitioner moves beyond the need to focus on external (exhalation) or internal (inhalation) breath, resulting in an effortless suspension of breath. Rather than just a technique, it is often described as a pause of consciousness where the mind becomes still, surpassing the limitations of time, place, and number.)

All yoga systems hold pranayama in high regard as a tool to control the mind and stop mental chatter. The initial steps of Ashtanga Yoga (Yama, Niyama, and Asana) function as essential preparation for Pranayama, while the subsequent limbs (Pratyahara, Dharana, Dhyana, Samadhi) constitute internal, meditative rituals. Devoted yoga practice can bring Self-realization in this lifetime itself. Because it is a powerful, precise, and scientific method, those seeking the ultimate goal of life follow Ashtanga Yoga.

Pranayama described in other Texts

Pranayama is the technique for quieting the mind, inducing tranquility and peace. When the breath (prana) wanders, the mind (chitta) is unsteady, but when the breath is stilled, the mind is also still. - Hatha Yoga Pradipika, Dwitheeyopaadesham 2 & 3.

By subduing latent impressions and controlling subtle breath fluctuations, the movements of the mind (chitta-vritti) can be stopped. - Hatha Yoga Pradipika.

Pranayama is the practice of controlling the breath to harmonize the two primary currents of vital energy: Prana (upward) and Apana (downward). – Yoga Yanjavalkyam.

When breath ceases, purity is attained. – Jabaladarsha-nopanishath.

The meaning of the word pranayama is to retain your breath for a specific time - Jabaladarshanopanishath.

Chitta (mind) is driven by latent impressions and subtle prana movements; controlling one regulates the other. Consequently, yogis practice pranayama to control the mind by regulating the breath/Prana. – Yoga Kundalini Upanishath.

Practitioners should balance their own breathing (process of inhalation and exhalation).

Pranayama is holding your inner life force within to stabilize it, allowing it to move inside you instead of letting it leave.

- Dhyanam, Dharana, Samadhi, Shri Venugopal S., Mathrubhumi Books

Awakening these energies is a feat for advanced yogis, achieved by Kumbhaka (breath retention) to guide prana through the nadis (nerves). – Kundalini Yoga Praveshika

Those who constantly practice breathe retention- whether walking or sitting, or all the time- never allowing it to escape, achieve a state of immortality. – Uthara Gita

Pranayama is mastered through the deliberate regulation of rechaka and Kumbhaka. - Swami Vivekananda

Contained within these statements are the secrets of Pranayama. Beyond daily practice, a sincere practitioner is advised to reflect on them often. Then, the hidden truth in each of these statements will be revealed automatically. Depending on a person's nature, one of these philosophies will act as their guiding inner light. For this reason, the secrets of Pranayama are shared here as much as possible. One only needs to approach these with a spirit of intense inquiry. Just as effortlessly as churning butter from yogurt, the deepest secrets and mysteries of Yoga will effortlessly unfold in front of us.

How to Practice Pranayama

Let us examine the practical application of Pranayama, guided by the foundational principles discussed so far.

The method to prolong Kumbhaka (Bahya sthambha Vruthi)

Use your right thumb and ring finger to close the nostrils, keeping the index and middle fingers straight.

Step 1: Close your right nostril with your thumb, and then exhale completely through the left nostril.

Step 2: Maintain your current position and take a slow, deep breath in through your left nostril, filling your lungs completely (poorakam).

Step 3: Gently close both nostrils and hold your breath for as long as you comfortably can, without straining (Anthara kumbhakam).

Step 4: Now, Gently take your thumb off the nostril and exhale fully through the right side (Rechakam).

Step 5: Close the nostrils and retain the breath out for some time (Rechaka Kumbhakam).

Step 6: Now, Remove your thumb, and then breathe in slowly through your right nostril (Poorakam).

Step 7: Close both nostrils and do Pooraka Kumbhaka (Anthara kumbhakam).

Step 8: Release the ring finger, and then slowly breathe out through the left side (Rechakam).

Step 9: Now, close both nostrils and hold your breath (Rechaka Kumbhakam).

Now you have completed one cycle of Pranayama. In the same order you can practice 7 or 14 cycles. This is regarded as a supreme technique, characterized by its immense potency. Through the practice of exhaling (Rechaka), holding the breath (Kumbhaka) or suspension of breath after exhalation (Bahyakumbhaka), the vital energy (Prana) enters Sushumna Nadi. This method of pranayama generates a tremendous amount of heat. Engage in Kriya practice gracefully and without exertion. Ensure this is practiced comfortably, avoiding any shortness of breath or shivering. Let the mind become fully absorbed in Kumbhakas – inhalation and exhalation. With consistent practice, the breath naturally becomes deep, slow, and subtle even during daily life, eventually culminating in a spontaneous state of effortless suspension known as Kevala Kumbhaka. This Pranayama technique requires achieving equilibrium across all four phases of breathing: controlled inhalation (Poorakam), internal retention (Antharakumbhakam), controlled exhalation (Rechakam), and external retention (Bahyakumbhakam) 1:4:2:1/2. If you inhale for a count of eight, you should hold the breath

(Antharakumbhakam) four times (32), exhale (Rechakam) 2 times (16), and hold empty (Bahya Kumbhaka) for count of four. Initial difficulty in maintaining this schedule is normal; consistency will bring improvement.

Those who practice only Porakam, Antharakumbhakam and Rechakam should practice @ 1:4:2. Focused point of view should be in between the eyebrows. Please adhere strictly to your Guru's guidance when practicing this technique.

Abhyanthara-sthambha-vruthi or Sidha Vidya, Hamsa Vidya

Abhyantara-Stambha-Vritti is a yogic technique that uses voluntary control (by place, time, and number) to make the natural inhalation and exhalation longer and more refined without force. It refers to the deliberate lengthening of the breath (dirgha) and increasing its subtlety (suksmah). Pranayama is performed in a stable seated position—such as Padmasana, Siddhasana, or Vajrasana, with the head and spine aligned vertically. With eyes softly open, gently direct your attention upward to the third eye centre (brow centre). To keep the nostrils open or close, fingers are not used at this stage. Hold your hands tight or in 'Chin Mudra'(the gesture of Consciousness). Inhale slowly and deeply through both nostrils. When the lungs are full, exhale slowly through both nostrils. Prioritize extending the duration of the exhale (Rechaka). Allow your breath to be natural and effortless. Breathing should be as natural and effortless as possible. While the nostrils are the entry point, effective breathing is primarily a throat-centered action. During inhalation, visualize breath entering through the Brahmarandhra, descending down the back of the throat and along the spine, ultimately reaching the Manipura chakra. Then, on the exhale, visualize the breath moving up the spine, through the back of the throat, and exiting above the Brahmarandra. Maintain absolute focus on the process. Where the mind goes, the Prana follows. Sustain this effort for as long as possible. You may notice your breath becoming deeper, longer, and nearly imperceptible. As a result, you will experience a greater sense of calm, inner quiet, and delight. Sincere Pranayama practice paves the way for the manifestation of higher yogic characteristics. This is just a rudimentary outline of Pranayama. The nuances and hidden procedures involved are not covered here. One can only master this after being initiated by a Guru. Only then will the Kriyas reach their full potential and bring effective results.

Mudras (gestures) and Bandhas (locks)

Mudra means "seal," and these gestures are primarily used in yoga practice to either block or redirect the flow of bio-energy (prana) within the body, directing it to specific areas where it is needed, or to complete and connect the circuits of prana flow. This action concurrently achieves a balance in the power of the Panchabhoota. Also, mudras are instrumental in maintaining single-pointed concentration and sustaining alertness throughout meditation, ensuring sleep does not interfere. Bandhas and mudras share almost identical functions. However, Bandhas (yogic techniques) are used to 'lock' prana in particular places, focusing energy for greater awareness. Explaining the techniques of Mudras and Bandhas will clarify the concepts.

It should be remembered that the practice of Pranayama is complete only when the bandhas and mudras are employed.

Key Mudras

Aswini Mudra, Maha Mudra, Mahavedha Mudra (Mahabhedam), Shambhavi Mudra, and Khechari Mudra are considered the prime mudras within various traditional yoga texts and practices. These specific mudras are often highlighted for their significant effects on the body's energy and consciousness.

Aswini Mudra

Method of application involves simultaneously inhaling (pooraka) through both nostrils (nadees) while contracting the muscles associated with the genitals. (It's like a cow tightens its sphincter muscles after passing dung). One should also tighten the sphincter muscles. Should maximize the duration of your breath-hold. Thereafter, slowly exhale the breath through the nostrils and relax the muscles. Aswini Mudra is used to divert the downward flow of prana so it can flow upward through the sushumna nadi.

Maha Mudra

Sit with your legs extended forward. Bend your right leg and place the heel in the perineum (the area between the genitals and anus), applying gentle and even pressure. Breathe in nasally, bend forward from the waist, and secure a grip on the left big toe using both hands. Maintain a slightly elevated head position and direct your gaze to a point between your eyebrows, holding this posture for as long as possible. Keep your abdomen expanded to the maximum. You can feel the prana shift from the Ida and Pingala channels and flow upward through Sushumna. This constitutes one cycle of the kriya. Repeat the process on the other side: bending the left leg and holding the right big toe, the same kriya can be repeated. Some people incorporate Moolabandha also simultaneously. However, it is found to be less than satisfactory.

Ashwini Mudra and Maha Mudra, due to the practice of Aantara Kumbhaka (internal breath retention), may elevate blood pressure and thus should be approached with extreme caution. Individuals with pre-existing hypertension or cardiovascular conditions should consult a qualified yoga instructor before attempting these practices.

Mahavedha Mudra (Mahabheda)

Perform this kriya in the same manner as you would practice Mahamudra, ensuring the breath is retained externally following a full exhale.

Sit with your legs extended forward. Bend your right leg and place the heel in the perineum (the area between the genitals and anus), applying gentle and even pressure. Breathe in nasally, bend forward from the waist, and secure a grip on the left big toe using both hands. Bring your chin down to touch your chest. Focus your gaze upon the bhrumadhya (the point between the eyebrows) and hold your breath externally (after exhaling) for as long as you comfortably can. Conclude the movement by releasing your hands and returning to the original position. Repeat the process on the other side: bending the left leg and holding the right big toe, the same kriya can be repeated. While performing Mahabheda mudra, there is a possibility of increased body heat. It is advisable to refrain from attempting this kriya if the pingala nadi is already active or overstimulated.

Shambhavi Mudra

To practice this, sit in one of several meditative postures - either Vajrasana, Siddhasana, or Padmasana - then inhale deeply through both nostrils to completely fill your lungs. Focus your gaze upon the bhrumadhya (the point between the eyebrows) and hold your breath as long as you comfortably can. Gently exhale while moving back to the initial posture. Perform this kriya repeatedly. This powerful, miraculous kriya is highly effective for easily activating the Ajna chakra.

Khechari Mudra

Close your eyes and assume any of the aforementioned asanas (postures). Fold your tongue backward so that the tip rests as far back on the soft palate (roof of the mouth) as possible. Slowly and fully inhale through both nostrils. Hold your breath for as long as you comfortably can (Antharkumbhakam). Breathe out slowly to return to your natural state. Pause briefly, then repeat the kriya.

Prana, ascends through the Sushumna Nadi, moving past the Vishuddhi and Ajna chakras, ultimately culminating its journey at the pineal gland, considered the central energetic point in the body.

Practising any of these Mudras alone can lead you to enlightenment. They are so powerful. Some practitioners perform these Mudras with pranayama

Pancha Kosha (Five Sheaths) doctrine

According to the Pancha Kosha theory, human existence is composed of five distinct, interconnected layers or sheaths, that veil the Self (Atman): Annamaya Kosha, Pranamaya Kosha, Manomaya Kosha, Vijnanamaya Kosha, and Anandamaya Kosha; order being gross level to subtle level. This sequence progresses inward from the external physical body to the innermost essence of bliss.

Annamaya Kosha, the "food-sheath is comprised of fundamental elements such as bone, marrow, and flesh, and is sustained entirely by the food and water we consume. In the body, there is a continuous flow of bio-current or Prana; a constant, underlying energetic movement within the physiological system. What is known as the Pranamaya Kosha is this energy body. Manomaya Kosha or mind sheath, is the layer of consciousness responsible for processing sensory input and transmitting these perceptions to the brain via the nervous system. It is the mental and emotional body that interprets the signals received from the five senses. This is the layer where energy or information is exchanged. The Vijnanamaya Kosha, the wisdom or intellect sheath is where information is analyzed, processed, and compared with existing knowledge, facilitating understanding and discernment. Anandamaya Kosha is the subtlest layer that serves as the foundation for all these activities. The Pancha Kosha theory can be easily understood by drawing an analogy to modern computer technology.

In this comparison, the physical components of a computer, such as the motherboard, CPU, and memory, represent the Annamaya Kosha.The flow and operation of electricity that powers these components is analogous to the Pranamaya Kosha.The most subtle layer, the abstract level of digital data and signals ("01"), corresponds to the Manomaya Kosha. CPU compares incoming data with data that was stored previously. These actions are being executed by the pre-existing program installed on the system. This entire arrangement can be regarded as the Vijnanamaya Kosha. This can be defined as our ego. The ego itself is the sole entity that both perceives and experiences the mental processes occurring within the Manomaya Kosha. These various gross layers are the manifestations of the Atma, which exists in a subtler state. Therefore, the Anandamaya Kosha is akin to the person who operates the computer. That is, the computer functions as an extension of the operator's human brain. Similarly, the four layers, namely Annamaya Kosha, Pranamaya Kosha, Manomaya Kosha, and Vijnanamaya Kosha, are the gross layers of Anandamaya Kosha, the Atma. All these are different layers of the Existence. The pancha koshas or five sheaths provide a layered model for the human being, analogous to the layers of the physical body (skin, fat, flesh, and bone.

Technique for opening Ajna Chakra or Third Eye

Across all paths, the fundamental purpose of Pranayama is to arouse the dormant Kundalini energy located at the base of the spine and guide it to ascend through the Sushumna nadi to the Sahasrara chakra. Thus, awakening the Ajna Chakra (third eye) is necessary for any pranayama technique to successfully channel energy to the Sahasrara (crown) chakra. However, certain techniques focus more directly on activating the Ajna Chakra.

Mindful awareness nourishes the awakening of the Ajna Chakra. The moment you fix your attention on the space between the eyebrows, that energy center begins to activate.

Yogis use the 'Eyebrow Center Gazing' technique of Shambhavi Mudra specifically for this purpose only. It involves gently focusing the eyes on the brow center to, in essence, "see" the inner self. When awakened, the Prana flowing through Ida and Pingala, converges and activates the Ajna chakra, which acts as their meeting point.

Yogis regularly practice Shambhavi Mudra as part of their Sidha Vidhya Pranayama. Inhale slowly and deeply through both nostrils, allowing your lungs to fill completely. Breathe out slowly through your nose taking twice as long as the inhale. That is, if you inhale to a count of 8, then exhale to a count of 16. This should be a slow quiet process. Maintain Khechari Mudra by keeping the mouth closed and continuously folding the tongue backward to touch the roof of the mouth or upper palate. This pranayama can be practiced as many times as you like. It has no side effects. Regular application of this, increases spiritual vitality.

Unlocking the vital secrets of Pranayama

Why do some people fail to experience benefits even after years of Pranayama practice?

The primary objective of pranayama is to harmonize the flow of prana throughout the nadis. Free circulation of prana along the spine brings both sides of the brain into equilibrium, fostering mental and emotional stability. This is the state of absolute, effortless absorption; Samadhi. Diverse factors often lead to obstructions in the body's extensive neural network. Through consistent practice Pranayama, the sadhaka removes restrictions to allow unobstructed prana circulation.

Practicing standard Pranayama activates and harmonizes the left (lunar) and right (solar) nadis, fostering equilibrium along the spine. So, nadis are activated uniformly, regardless of whether they were previously blocked or open. Although both energy channels are active, the uneven flow of prana between them continues. For instance, if the initial energetic flow of the Ida (lunar/left) nadi is 10 units and Pingala (solar/right) is 12 units, performing standard Pranayama techniques typically elevates both, changing their respective energy levels to 11 and 13 volts. Because the two-unit energy imbalance remains, the inner system has not achieved harmony. As a result, the practitioner fails to experience any inner transformation.

A sadhaka should only focus on specific kriyas that activate dormant or blocked energy channels within their system, so that the blocks are removed and the nadis on both sides are balanced. At this juncture, regular Pranayama unlocks significant, life-altering benefits for the practitioner. That is, each Sadhaka should adopt customized pranayama routines to suit his individual spiritual and physical development. At this stage, it is necessary to have a Guru who is proficient in teaching these Kriyas. Only a qualified one can accurately assess your internal energy level and recommend specific Pranayama and Mudras to bring it into balance.

How to Evaluate the Long-Term Viability and Impact of a Method for Your Unique Circumstances

A vast human population inhabits the planet. While universal principles govern human physiology and psychology, individual physical and mental conditions are highly idiosyncratic. Therefore, the efficacy of a method, deemed suitable for one individual may prove ineffective for another. Self-realization is pursued through a range of techniques across various yoga streams. A comprehensive study of all options is impractical and not required. As all paths guide toward the ultimate goal of Self-realization, choose the Pranayama and Kriyas best suited for your physical and mental state, and commit to continuous practice. Failure to do so may jeopardize your health and delay your progress. This could potentially impede progress towards the final objective. Here is why a capable Guru matters most. An experienced Guru provides personalized guidance based on a thorough assessment of each disciple. Everyone can select a suitable path based on their own experiences. The selection is based on observing the unique inner experiences of each practitioner during their practice.

It is recommended to practice each kriya for at least three consecutive days. Experiencing both inner calm and physical ease suggests, the practice is appropriate. Performing kriyas that don't match your body or mind can cause harm, making guidance from a capable Guru crucial for avoiding negative effects. Side effects can include anxiety, depression, or physical strain or emotional instability. When you engage in practices that align with you, happiness and vitality flow naturally. Whereas, practices inducing fatigue, listlessness, or disquiet are inappropriate.

As yoga practitioners gain expertise, they develop the ability to discern the effectiveness of a kriya. The subtle nuances of the kriya will become clear to him from the very first attempt. With his experience, he can select the best path and move forward rapidly. This is the correct approach.

It is no secret that what you consume directly impacts your mind. The psychological impacts of drinking alcohol are experienced by the drinkers themselves. In a similar fashion, using drugs and other stimulants impacts the mind. Those who use certain substances may experience conditions similar to those traditionally achieved by a yogi, temporarily. Despite the effects of liquor or drugs being transient, people still go after them because they will momentarily experience happiness. As the effects wear off, their mental state will plummet to a level worse than it was before consumption. Ultimately, resorting to such contrived methods for fleeting pleasure will lead to self-destruction and the realization of goal will be jeopardized forever.

When Yoga practices increases the body temperature

Yoga practices -especially specific Pranayama methods- work to increase the body's fire. Digestion happens in the abdomen, located in the middle of the body. The energy vital for the existence of life is produced here. The processes of digestion, conversion of food into nutrients, assimilation in the bloodstream, and elimination of waste products are exclusively centered here. Abdomen can be compared as a biological nuclear reactor, converting physical matter into fuel. Immense heat is generated both in nuclear reactors and in the abdomen.

According to Yoga, the fire that sustains life resides in the abdomen. Those who are sensitive enough can feel the fire in themselves. At times, one might have experienced the presence of a blazing inner fire. Invisible radiation is a known byproduct of using computers and mobile devices. This radiation often causes a distinct burning sensation that is similar to what we experience in the abdominal region.

Yoga practices, especially Pranayama, are designed to kindle the inner fire, driving the flames upward to transcend the Vishuddhi chakra. By stimulating the inner fire through pranayama, the energy ascends to the Sahasrara, inducing a flow of bliss that marks the moment of spiritual awakening. Vigorous pranayama techniques - specifically Bhastrika and Kapalabhati—along with Nadi Shuddha and Anuloma Viloma, generate internal heat and stimulate the body. Various Pranayama techniques are practiced to clear nadis, enabling the free flow of vital life force. Since it is the virtuous function of Pranayama to kindle fire and extent of its reach upwards, the practitioner who is a seeker of Spirituality must do practice various Pranayama methods every day, without fail.

Because yogis mostly reside in the cold Himalayan hills, the heat generated by their Pranayama practices is a necessary benefit rather than a concern. Moreover, they survive the extreme cold weather by raising body heat by special Pranayama methods. However, the situation is different in the plains. In areas like ours, where it is hot most of the year, the internal heat generated by Pranayama can make life difficult.

Prolonged pranayama practices increase body heat, which may cause health issues such as skin disorders, hair loss, sleep deprivation, and reduced concentration. Diseases resulting from increased bile levels may affect the practitioner.

To manage this, practitioners generally adopt measures such as restricting pranayama to the morning, reducing practice duration, and minimizing heat generating methods. Some people apply oil to their head or take a bath before practice.

Practicing Pranayama methods that reduce body heat helps control your temperature. Controlling body temperature can be achieved by practicing Sheetali Pranayama and Agnisar Kriya. These techniques that are practiced by inhaling and exhaling through mouth reduce body heat. Pranayama balances the three doshas (Vata, Pitta, and Kapha). Each Pranayama is related to one of the three doshas. Practitioners should choose the method best suited to their body type and prioritize that practice. Those methods that are generally described may not suitable for everyone. One must determine the best method through intense observation or guidance from a competent Guru.

Brahmacharya

Throughout history, the profound concept of Brahmacharya -defined as aligning one's conduct with the Divine (Brahman) and mastering the senses - has been largely misinterpreted. It is a common assumption that all practitioners, regardless of gender, should remain celibate. It is held that absolute sexual abstinence is the only path to high spiritual attainment, and lapses are viewed as fatal to one's progress. They believe sexual intimacy drains energy and that cravings for it lead to mental instability. Brahmacharya (or in a broader sense, voluntary celibacy/chastity) is emphasized in specific Indian ascetic traditions and Christian monastic communities, based on this thought process.

Yogashastra (specifically classical/Raja Yoga) and Tantrik Science (Tantra) offer distinct approaches to self-realization. In Tantric science, the Panchamakaras - alcohol, meat, fish, grain (or gestures), and sexual union - are considered as ritual tools to achieve spiritual liberation. Rather than being forbidden, these are utilized to harness and sublimate raw energy into higher consciousness. Furthermore, these are the core tools of their spiritual practices. Practitioners of Tantric sadhana use ritualized intercourse as a specialized form of worship. This involves distinctive, conscious participation in sexual activity. Normally, sexual intimacy creates an overwhelming internal experience that makes a person lose track of him. Common sexual acts draw energy down into lower chakras, acting as the antithesis of the upward flow required to reach the highest states of awareness. Those practicing Tantra engage in sex as a meditative act, remaining consciously aware of every sensation and movement. He stays mindful of the subtle energy flowing from the start of the interaction. He observes the crescendo of the act and how their energies intertwine. Furthermore, they take special care to conserve energy by practicing internal ejaculation control. Thus, practitioners of Tantra vidya fulfill the requirements of Brahmacharya through a specialized, unique approach. Any worldly act when done with complete awareness becomes thantrik spiritual sadhana.

Yogis hold a different perspective: they believe that semen loss directly causes a depletion of vital force (prana), which can cause a practitioner to lose their elevated spiritual state and fall from their path. However, they believe that practicing self-imposed Brahmacharya will be detrimental rather than beneficial. They also discovered that trying to forcibly control the powerful, overwhelming flow of sexual energy can cause adverse physical and mental side effects. Restrictions stimulate curiosity and desire. Endocrine-generated sex hormones significantly influence the physical and mental state of any practitioner of yoga. Due to its influence, sexual desires are bound to arise in a yogi. However, they do not attempt to manage rising sexual desires through the practice of Brahmacharya. Yoga path advises practitioners to acknowledge desires, let them run their course, and transcend them to reach a higher state of being. For practitioners focused on conserving spiritual energy, the recommendation is to engage in sexual intimacy once in sixteen days. The fact that a significant number of revered Rishis lived within society; fulfilling familial duties while attaining high levels of consciousness itself is validation of above recommendation. In Hindu mythology and literature, there are indeed several prominent narratives where ascetics (rishis/munis) are distracted by the beauty of women, resulting in a loss of their accumulated spiritual energy. It shows that, repression is not a solution for a Yogi; sexual energy that is forcefully bottled up will erupt given the right circumstances, reverting to its instinctual outlet. Their life shows that no yogic attainment can match the power of that energy.

Beyond mere moderation, specific practices exist to convert raw sexual energy into spiritual awareness while simultaneously reducing the body's internal generation of that energy. Dedicated practice of specific Pranayama and kriyas for Self-realization facilitates the sublimation of sexual energy, leading to a gradual natural decline in libido and hormone production. Thus, Brahmacharya becomes a natural state, free from any strain. It is no longer just a ritual at that stage. It becomes second nature.

Lamas—regardless of gender—perform dedicated practices in monasteries for this specific purpose. Female ascetics engaged in deep spiritual disciplines often experience the permanent cessation of menstruation. Male lamas transmute their innate biological energy into higher spiritual consciousness by channeling it upward, bypassing the arousal of sexual desire. Rather than battling sexuality, yoga approaches it through moderation or by elevating this vital energy to higher levels. This is authentic Brahmacharya in action.

The true nature of cosmic illusion (MAYA – the material world)

The concept of "Maya Darshana," or cosmic illusion, is Indian philosophy's most debated idea, often misunderstood and ridiculed through humorous tales, leading to endless commentaries that question its very essence. Youngsters who are exposed to funny stories (perhaps misinterpretations or satirical versions of ancient Indian texts like Puranas or fables), are developing disrespect, scorn, and a tendency to ridicule traditional Indian philosophies and wisdom, seeing them as silly rather than profound. Those who misunderstand or intentionally distort these philosophies are spreading false stories.

Indian yoga philosophy is founded on the profound insights attained through deep meditation by enlightened seers. Through deep meditative absorption (Samadhi), they perceived universal truths, achieving the highest levels of awareness with their inner vision. Therefore, to truly understand these insights, ordinary people must raise themselves above their current level of ignorance. True wisdom awakens only when we put their spiritual insights into action (practice), even if just a little. As spiritual practice deepens, a practitioner gains a clearer, more profound understanding of spiritual realities, moving from ordinary perception to the enlightened perspective of a seer. We will truly understand the depth of their teachings when we reach their level of spiritual attainment. Mere reading or listening provides only theoretical, superficial knowledge; failing to reach the core essence of the subject. True understanding requires personal experience. Also, those people will proclaim their hypotheses as reality in public forums. These types of explanations contribute significantly to the marginalization of the Maya theory. Many prevalent accounts of Maya are merely intellectual exercises, lacking the depth of direct, spiritual insight. Let's start by reviewing what is commonly understood about Maya theory.

Their view is that this life is a fabric of deceptions - a myth that veils the truth and therefore the world does not exist. Since the world is a projection, then everything we experience is fundamentally mythological. It is non-existent. They say, Maya is like a dream or a mirage—it feels real while you are experiencing it, but it has no permanent existence. Since the container (the world) is unreal, the contents are likewise unreal. Since the individual self, the physical body, and the cycle of existence are all illusions, the sensations of pleasure and pain are likewise non-existent. Therefore, understand that this existence is merely a transient illusion. That is detachment; keeping a level of equanimity. God is the only self-existent Being. Wisdom is, identifying the one and only truth that transcends time. So, these people have formulated Maya doctrine, in an entirely flawed and ridiculous manner. There is story to narrate:

Pretending to be enlightened, a monk went around proclaiming that everything around is an illusion. People adored him as a great sage. Word of his fame and reputation reached the king. The king sought to examine the monk. He invited him to the Palace.

Oh, great soul," the King inquired, "what constitutes the substance of this world? Enlighten me, I pray, regarding the Eternal Truth you have discovered."

The learned person told the Maharaja, who stood humbly before him thus: "My child, this entire world is but an illusion; a mere projection of the mind. God alone is the ultimate truth. Direct your search only towards Him."

The King humbly asked, "You mean you, me, and this life, this palace are all an illusion?"

Caressing his beard the knowledgeable person replied, "Yes, everything is deception only," he categorically confirmed.

"If that is so, you must be prepared for a test," the King demanded. "Only then can we assimilate your wisdom."

Having no other alternative, he had to agree for the test.

He was placed in the center of the courtyard and confronted with a charging elephant in musth, prompting a desperate scramble for safety.

As he fled, the King persistently questioned him: “Is this all just an illusion? If everything is, then this elephant must be, too! Why run from it?”

“True, but that’s just my awareness; the elephant doesn’t know it,” he replied, without breaking stride.

While the story was seen as undeniable proof that Maya doctrine was untrue, it actually was only a wrong interpretation of the theory.

Now, let us look at what the Great Sages have to say about the nature of Maya. While not exhaustive, we will examine two interpretations that are widely accepted. Understanding this will allow us to comprehend the logical, correct theories propounded by holy sages. Both interpretations accept the world and its happenings, just through different means.

In the first view, the physical realm is identified as being constituted by material substances. It manifests on both subtle and gross levels. All of us are part of it. Existence is manifested in both material mass and energetic fields. It manifests subtly as the finest physical particles, appearing as atoms and molecules, yet fundamentally exists as energy beyond form. Although the world appears to us as solid matter, at its most fundamental level, the world also exists in the form of energy at the subtlest level. The fundamental nature of the universe is characterized by the constant mass-energy equivalence and interconversion. True Maya lies in recognizing the unchanging reality, rather than dwelling on the world of constant flux.

The second Maya doctrine states that sensory perception does not reflect true reality. Light from a star located five light-years away takes five years to reach us. Because the star is five light-years away, we are seeing it in the form and place it held five years in the past. Our perception of the universe is a glimpse into its past. The light from distant objects took billions of years to reach Earth, but our minds process this ancient light as the present, a 'real' universe. Many of the stars we see now actually may have already reached the end of their lifecycles. This implies that our sensory experience is ultimately a manifestation of Maya.

The first doctrine of Maya is failing to recognize the ephemeral nature of the phenomenal world, while the second doctrine defines it as the inability to perceive the absolute reality of the present moment. Nevertheless, both doctrines are grounded in the reality of the world.

A third viewpoint, based on the same facts, more accurately reflects reality by interpreting Maya according to the vision of the Sages. Rather than viewing Maya as a conundrum regarding the universe's existence, their interpretation defines it as a distortion of how we perceive the world. This underscores the constraints of our analytical capabilities. We perceive the objective reality of the world by experiencing it through our senses and interpreting it with our intellect. For instance, light rays reflect off an object and reach our eyes, stimulating the retina. The brain then processes this signal, allowing us to see the object. Here, there is an external object, an intellect that perceives it, and the internal representation (or mental image) generated by that perception.

Object – individual mind or intellect – the reflection of object; we can illustrate this reality in a straightforward manner. The relationship between the observer (mind) and the observed (object) is simple, that the mind creates a mental image or reflection of the external reality. Here, the observer of the world acts as a mirror, reflecting its reality. This individual is driven by tendencies. I.e., the reflected image of the world is quite subjective. The image will be the same colour as the mirror. Then, we accept the reality evident to our intellect. This is Maya. Therefore, the Sages did not define the world itself as Maya; rather, it is the reflected colored image and the intellect that mistakenly believe it so. In other words, we don't perceive the world objectively; instead, our minds act as a filter. When this filter changes (as our mindset evolves), our perception of the world transforms accordingly. It is the tinted veil/covering of perception that hangs between the universe and the known universe (to us). We can only perceive true Reality once the veil of illusion is lifted.

To understand this clearly, one should know what are impressions/tendencies are; the subconscious imprints left by past actions, thoughts, and experiences that shape a person's behavior, personality, and reactions (often referred to as Samskaras or Vasanas in Yoga psychology). In contemporary terms, this is referred to as genetic programming. Our genetics synchronize the operations of our physical, mental, and intellectual faculties. We all function according to our own specially encrypted, internal systems. These behavioral patterns function as karmic operating systems. Every deed is registered in the karmic database at a subtle level. At death, the hardware perishes, but the operating system simply reboots in a new machine. This defines your next reincarnation. To say, one takes birth with this operating system carried over from one birth to another is referred as vasanas in the ancient yoga context.

A person's body, mind, and intellect function entirely based on their underlying vasanas. To elucidate this, an example that corroborates the Theory of Evolution can be denoted. For over a hundred years, the dense forests of Africa have been the site of a brutal slaughter, where elephants were relentlessly hunted for their ivory, a commodity that nearly caused the extinction of their species. Tusks became the reason for elimination of their race itself. As a result, the propensity for tusk development in newborn calves decreased. Nature inherently prepared the necessary genetic framework. This perfectly illustrates how vasanas are passed down to future generations.

Disorganized mental states stem from deeply ingrained tendencies, with each mind tuned to its own specific wavelength. When the mind and intellect that reflect the world are unsteady, the reflection itself shakes. When the mind is still and thoughts cease in samadhi, the reflection stops shaking, allowing it to reflect Reality exactly as it is. This is perception of Ultimate Truth - Sathya Darshana. With the cessation of vasanas, the wandering mind ceases its distractions and achieves stillness. At that moment, Yogi in Samadhi state experiences Reality firsthand; because only the enlightened ones know the Ultimate Reality (Brahman). Therefore the quest for Self-realization is inherently a quest for Absolute Reality.

www.ingramcontent.com/pod-product-compliance
Lightning Source LLC
Chambersburg PA
CBHW050018170726
48282CB00025B/450
9789358123722